Dear M,

Wishing you more and more of joy as your read what of God has shown me, as I am and studied His Word.

Love you So Much Mijo,
Your Tia,
Crusita

Speak God's Language

And He will open the doors to Blessings

by Crusita Sosa

FORWARD

The writing of this book is for the Glory of God. It is because of Him, His love, guidance, leading, and direction that I have taken pen to paper.

God has given me a vision. A study on, " The power of The Tongue " or to be even more descriptive, " The Power of Blessing. " We are going to take a journey together that will help us to apply God's Word in our daily lives.

I have been walking with the Lord for 45 years. Through those years Holy Spirit taught me to observe what the affect of my words did to those around me and how they affect my environment, either for the good or for the bad.
In reflecting on the consequences, I began to write the results down and because of that, the birth of this book came to fruition. We have a God given power to either bless or curse our individual lives, the lives of our children, and others around us.

May God bless you as you take this journey with me.

ACKNOWLEDGEMENTS

The reality of this book has been largely due to the encouragement of my lifelong friend and husband, Felix who has practiced the life of blessing along with me. We are both grateful for our four children- Tony, Tammy, Linda, and Roy for being the wonderful blessings to us, as well as each of our sons and daughters-in-law. They have blessed us with ten beautiful grandchildren who are and have been brought up in the way of The Lord. The way of blessing. They are walking in the blessing and favor of God.

I am thankful for well-timed friends like Danny and Diana Hahlbohm, whose gentle encouragement led me to take the first steps to take this message out to others. I also want to thank Patty Burdette, whom I met through Diana. After reading my rough drafts she offered her services to edit my book. I am so very grateful to her and the time she took to help me. Thank you Patty, your creative skills will be enjoyed by many for years to come. And thank you Danny for your beautiful art work on the cover and Diana for your time in putting it all together for me. As well as your love, prayers, and support.

Thank you to my sister, Carmy Burkett for your love, prayers, and support also. You have always been a very special blessing in my life, and I give God thanks for you.

Personal Reviews:

"When you meet Crusita, you are meeting a child of the King. Not a prima dona, but someone of royal priesthood of her Lord, Jesus Christ. Quietly she shares her blessings, and you truly miss out if you do not learn to listen. What she shares is not of her soul, but the Holy Spirit to her spirit connection. Those of us who call her friend are blessed, indeed."

Kathleen McNear Smith,
Published Author and writer.

"I have been a Christian and follower of Jesus Christ for over 20 years yet never realized the power of actually "Blessing" another by word and thought. Crusita has opened my eyes into a new learning of the Word regarding 'blessings'. Truly, a wonderful teaching."

Danny Hahlbohm,
world renown artist and founder of inspired-art.com.

"Although I have not known Crusita over an extended period of time, she is a woman after the heart of God. Crusita is a "Blesser"! I met Crusita about six months ago through a divine appointment with my beloved friend, Diana Hahlbohm. It has been my privilege to read and edit the teaching lessons that Crusita is presenting to the body of Christ at such a time as this. However, these lessons are crucial in bringing victory in life to everyone, not just those in the body of Christ! I gleaned tremendously in my own life of the truth nuggets explaining the difference between blessing and cursing. Praise God, I have seen such positive changes in very important relationships, as I have chosen to be a blesser!!!"

Patty Burdette,
book publication editor.

All rights reserved. No part of this publication (text or images) may be reproduced, stored in a retrieval system, or transmitted in any form or by any means electronic, mechanical, photocopy, computer, or any other except for brief quotations of written material in printed reviews, without permission in writing from the author.

Printed in the United States of America.
© 2017 Crusita Sosa

Website: wwww.lightofeden.com

Email: fcsosa@comcast.net

Unless otherwise noted, all scripture quotations are from the
KING JAMES VERSION (KJV): public domain.

Scripture quotations marked (NIV) are taken from the
THE HOLY BIBLE, NEW INTERNATIONAL VERSION ®.
Copyright© 1973, 1978, 1984, 2011 by Biblica, Inc.TM.
Used by permission of Zondervan.

Scripture quotations marked "NASB" are taken from the
New American Standard Bible, Copyright 1960, 1962,
1963, 1971, 1972, 1973, 1975, 1977, 1995 by
The Lockman Foundation. Used by permission.

Scripture quotations marked (NKJV) are taken from the
NEW KING JAMES VERSION®. Copyright © 1982 by Thomas
Nelson. Used by permission. All rights reserved.

TABLE OF CONTENTS

1. Power Of The Tongue..09
2. Blessings Revealed..17
3. Faith..23
4. The Blessing We Inherit...31
5. According To God...36
6. Do It God's Way..51
7. The Aaronic Blessing...60
8. Which One Are You?..74
9. He Is Pitching His Tent..80
10. It Is Our Choice...89
11. The Heart Of God's Kingdom................................95
12. The United Church..103
13. The Commanded Blessing....................................112
14. Who Is Ruling?...120
15. Resurrection Power..134
16. A House Blessed..142
17. A Hedge Of Blessing...148
18. The Blessings Of Forgiveness.............................158
19. Bless Yourself..170
20. Our Heavenly Father Is A Blesser......................179

CHAPTER 1

THE POWER OF THE TONGUE

God has given me a vision. A study on, " The Power of The Tongue " or to be even more descriptive, "The Power of Blessing". We are going to take a journey together that will help us to apply God's Word in our daily lives. To apply the power and the promise of His blessings in our individual lives, the lives of our children, and others around us.

But first, let us pause a moment to really understand what the word blessing means, or The Act of Blessing.

To Bless, for a Christian is much more then a word. It is walking in the demonstration of God's love toward others, in thought, word and deed from His perspective.

I have a friend who I have been sharing these lessons with and she too, is finding breakthrough in relationships by applying an active stance of blessing. Lynn has felt a distance between herself and her daughter-in-law for years. In the past she has been in a more critical inner stand. After reading a few of the lessons she began to think and pray blessing over her daughter-in-law instead of projecting anger or disappointment in her.

Lynn began to feel such a change in her own heart, while at the same time noticing a softening taking place in her daughter-in-law. Soon they began to receive one another in a more open and heartfelt way, less guarded and more loving. What makes this so precious is that this change has come right at the perfect time, as the daughter-in-law is now pregnant with the only grandchild Lynn will ever have. God longs for us to be giving and receiving blessings in order that He can bestow upon us the richness of all His Blessings. Once we open that door we are destined to experience divine change. The results of blessing someone or a situation will always bring good results because it is the very word of God in action.

God, our heavenly Father has given us many keys on how to walk in the fullness of His kingdom. Our tongue and how we use it, what we choose to speak, or not speak opens or close's doors of blessings or curses in our life, and the lives of those around us.

"Death and life are in the power of the tongue: and they that love it shall eat the fruit thereof." Prov.18: 21

Now we come to what the word Curse or the act of

cursing actually means: To curse someone is to walk in the total opposite of God's perspective toward others in thought, word, and deed. He looks at all of us through His eyes and heart with pure love for everyone.

There are thoughts that are rich, and bring wealth to the inner man. Then there are thoughts that steep in a cup of poverty and to sip on them only brings about desolation. Now these are mere thoughts, imagine when the thoughts turn into words and we not only rule the inner roost of our own interior; we begin to change the course of those around us.

Oh Lord, we come before you now, and ask that you serve us a menu of Blessing, Truth and Revelation. Open our mind, and hearts to the teaching you have placed before us. Amen

> Have you ever asked yourself or others?
> 1) Why aren't there more healings?
> 2) Why are we struggling with our finances?
> 3) Why are our marriages falling apart?
> And so many other whys?

What We Speak

There is power in what we speak. What we choose to allow coming out of our mouths. To think before we speak and to ask ourselves, will this that I choose to speak create a blessing or a curse to the hearer?

POWER OF THE TONGUE

"If any man among you seems to be religious and bridleth not his tongue, but deceiveth his own heart, this man's religion is vain." James 1:26

(Bridle- Webster's dictionary) to restrain or control, as in a horse's bridle.

"Whoso keepeth his mouth and his tongue keepeth his soul from troubles." Prov. 21:23

I have heard said, " We have what we speak (our own thoughts), instead of speaking what we have. (His thoughts). We can have the fullness of the promises of God, if we speak and walk according to His Word. After all, didn't He give us dominion?

How did God create? (Gen.1: 3) And God said; 1:5, And God called; 1:6, And God said; 1:8 And God called; 1:9, And God said; 1:10, And God called; 1:24, And God said; Gen. 1:20, And God said; 1:24, And God said. Need I go on? In all of these verses, there is one factor that is the same. There was a spoken Word by God.

The Blessing Revealed

We are going to discover the different aspects of blessing. Most of us usually think of blessing in the scope of materialism. But, it is more than that. It's about a lifetime of blessing that causes changes in the hearts of those we bless as well as ourselves. The blessing I am referring to is more along the lines of prophetic declaration. Blessing, when understood from the perspective of the Creator of the universe, is creative restorative. We can see plainly that from the scriptures that our Heavenly Father is the redemptive God who delights in bringing things back into His divine order.

Through learning how to bless we can be a part of the redemptive process. The lifestyle of the blessing may be at times contrary to our human nature, but it is very much in agreement with the divine nature of God.

As we apply this lesson of blessing, we will be able to change our perspective of life itself and how we see others.

" You will know the truth and the truth will make you free." John 8:32

The reality of this verse is that the only truth that will make us free is not the truth that we hear but the truth we speak and apply. The subject of truth will be a strategic part of these lessons of " Blessing ".

Truth in scripture is different from what most would call truth. We would probably define truth as correct information. The bible definition is more in line with reality from God's perspective. Jesus described Himself as " The Way, The Truth, and The Life". So we can conclude that truth is an observation from Christ's point of view.

POWER OF THE TONGUE

In our court system, here in the U.S., a person would place his right hand on the bible and he or she would be asked, " Do you swear to tell the truth, the whole truth and nothing but the truth, so help you God?"

What they were really saying was that if they spoke the fullness of the truth, God would back them up. If not, then God couldn't because He is Truth, and cannot lie or else He would be going against His own Word.

It's the same with us in our daily lives. If we speak truth that is in line with God's Word, we are blessing an individual, but if we speak a negative or degrading word over someone, we are going contrary to the Word of God and we are stopping Him from blessing us, because we are cursing instead of blessing.

When the twelve spies' entered the land of Canaan to bring back the report of the Promised Land, they returned with various perspectives on what they saw. They reported to Moses that the land was just as God had promised. There were houses they would not have to build, vineyards they would not have to plant, and wells they would not have to dig. Ten of the spies reported that the sons of Anak were there, and they were giants. The two other spies, Joshua and Caleb, the sons of Anal, reported the same view of the land except they saw it through the truth that God had said, while the others stated what they saw through only facts.

POWER OF THE TONGUE

Facts seen by their eyes, for example, outward physical manifestations such as diseases. But truth is the way things appear through the eyes of God.

One of the principle points in our lessons is the contrast between facts and truth. Something may be factual but not necessarily truthful or " full of truth". God told the Israelites the land was theirs. The ones who saw the land through God's eyes eventually were able to inherit the land. The ten who saw the promise of God through circumstantial facts died without ever entering into their rest of inheritance.

Blessing will at times seem to be factually impossible, but we will inherit God's blessings and intended favor if we continue to speak blessing.

It is my hope that as we take this journey together we will see the importance of children receiving blessing from their fathers.

My prayer is that, as we learn together, the Holy Spirit will give us this God given ability to bless and empower us to live out His Truth in every part of our lives.

Lord, may the eyes of understanding be opened, and may we come into the full hope of the calling of You Lord. We speak and declare a blessing over this household of faith. We thank you for the power to bless. We choose to be on the mountain of blessing and declare Your blessing over our Your church. We thank You for your church, for its place in the community. We bless this city and may we be a light here. Whatever we do, let us express the love of Christ. Let the power of blessing come through our mouths everyday, on the job, over our families, wherever we are, and whomever we are around. Let our mouths only speak life. We thank You for the gift God have given us to bless and not curse. We bless you with relationships that build you up and do not tear down. May you be able to see farther into your destiny than ever before! We bless you with the peace of God to control every thought and the fear of God to establish your feet. May we be a blessing to you and may we be able to receive blessing from you. Amen

CHAPTER 2

BLESSINGS REVEALED

Inside each and everyone of us in the body of Christ is the ability to effect change in our environment as well as in our circumstances. What did Jesus say about the " mountains " that stand in our way?

"Truly I say to you, whoever says to this mountain, be taken up and cast into the sea and does not doubt in his heart, but believes that what he says is going to happen, it will be granted him." Mark 11:23

We have been given the power to bring about change to our environment and in our circumstances. What did God say to man in the first chapter of Genesis? Didn't He say that man has dominion? That is to say that man has the power or authority to rule. The power that has been given to us is dispersed through the words that we speak. The word " power " according to the Merriam Webster Dictionary, is " the ability to act or produce an effect." So, when we partner up with the will of our Heavenly Father as He has set forth in His Word, aligning our words with His that we speak; then we can experience the transforming power of blessing! Let's begin.

The Blessing Revealed

A parent, a close friend, or a relative can have such a great impact on our formation. How we speak to our husbands, wives, children; Do our words edify or tear down? The impact of these experiences will vary in degree, depending on the weightiness of the relationship. Even then, knowing our calling and destiny can be a struggle. It is enough of a struggle that many pass through life without ever really knowing why on earth they were placed here. There is a calling greater than any profession we choose. It is even greater than being called an apostle, prophet, evangelist, pastor, teacher or any other spiritual gift. Peter's letter makes this calling clear.

> *"Finally, all of you be of one mind, having compassion for one another; love as brothers, be tender-hearted, be courteous, not returning evil for evil or reviling for reviling, but on the contrary blessing; knowing that you were called to this, that you may inherit a blessing."* 1 Peter 3;8-9 NKJV

So simple and uncomplicated, but filled with expectation. What we are called to do is to bless and to receive the blessing. Discovering the power that is in the blessing will open up a whole new world of thinking and living. Blessing, and its counterpart, cursing, will set a path for us without our being fully aware of it. The name God gave Jesus is a called name. (Philippians 2:9-10) "For this reason also, God highly exalted Him, and bestowed on Him the name which is above every name, so that at the name of Jesus every knee will bow, of those who are in Heaven and on the earth and under the earth." Jesus was named and marked for the purpose of blessing and for the defending of those cursed. He became the Savior of God's creation from the curse. When we name our children, we should pray and ask God what to call them. We name them for the purpose of distinction and identification. What we name them can be prophetic for our child's future. Basically, we are saying over them, "This is your destiny and it is who you are; this is the value of your life."

A Clear And Plain Word

"Bad company corrupt good morals." 1 Cor.15:33

Let's stop here for just a moment to consider the people you hang out with.

(1) How influential have they been in determining where you are and what you are doing today?

(2) What about the environment you live in and the environment you grew up in as a child? Did it have any bearing on where you are and who you are?

(3) How are you impacting the people you associate with? Are you a positive or negative influence?

(4) How might you apply the power of blessing to change your own environment and the lives of others you come in contact with?

BLESSINGS REVEALED

You were called... the word "called" in (1 Peter 3:8-9) is "Kaleo". It is a very strong word that is similar to the choosing of a person's name. We know that the name that our parents, family, friends, and even society have labeled us can have a profound effect upon our future. So then, ask yourself, who are you? Have you been labeled by friends, family, or society? Have other people's perceptions of who you are affected your own self-image. People often lack the insight of being able to see you as God sees you. Who does God say that you are? God does not see you through the eyes of imperfection or lack. He does not see your mistakes or your shortcomings. God sees you perfect, whole, and complete in Him. He sees you (prophetically) as He called you to be, to be also as complete in the future, as He created you. Not what you or others see you as now.

"For I know the plans I have for you, declares (speaks, proclaims) the Lord, plans for your welfare, and not for calamity to give you a future and a hope." Jeremiah 29:11

In His eyes, we are a perfect, and complete creation in Him.

The next time you hear someone respond to a sneeze with "Bless You", stop to consider what that response might actually mean. "God Bless You!" People say that all the time and consider that to be blessing someone. Not really, it's more than that. Saying "bless you", has become such a common salutation or spirited filler for any occasion, that the power of blessing is lost and remains untapped. It's much more than a mere formality. Blessing has the power to turn lives around and make us into a blesser. True blessing spoken over someone or something (such as finances etc.) is describing the way God sees them. This is a prophetic insight to see the way someone or something is supposed to be, not how they may appear to be at the moment. So, when we talk about blessing someone, we are prophetically stating, "May the Lord grant you all of His intention for you", or "May God's full expectation for you be fulfilled in your life". And we know that God's intentions for people are good. Take a short trip to Jeremiah 29:11 or revisit the first few chapters of Genesis.

These speak of the heart of God toward us, His creation. When we speak blessings over our children, as Jacob did, we are saying what their life should be. (Genesis 49: 28) Jacob was not stating the condition of his children at the moment, but what they would be. If you follow Jacob's sons throughout scripture, it is obvious they followed the prophetic path of the blessing of their father.

God's intentions aren't based on whether the one receiving the blessing has the right attitude. It has nothing to do with how we feel, and everything to do with how God wants it to be or how He sees it. What a radically different response from what we naturally tend to do! It is no surprise when our prayers are more of a reporting nature than a praying for the solution. We are good at reporting the doctor's diagnosis, the conditions surrounding a situation, and so on. Precious time is wasted when we continually rehearse the disaster that will occur if God does not come through in a situation. It is with the eyes of faith that we look at the situation through God's

BLESSINGS REVEALED

intended purpose and His perspective.

CHAPTER 3

FAITH

Speaking of faith, let's check out Proverbs.

(Proverbs 28:20).
"A faithful man will abound with blessings..."

We usually interpret this as a faithful man will receive blessing, but the structure of this sentence means that a man of faith will be full of blessing. To be " full " of blessing is in us to give away. We receive it from the Father so we can give it out. We cannot give away what we do not have, and if God says we can bless, then it must be in us to give. The same thing is true of forgiveness. Like blessing, it is a gift that we can either give or hold on to.

A Spiritual Principle

FAITH

Whatever we sow will set a measurement of return. Needing mercy from God? Then give mercy. Want blessing? Release blessing. If you don't want to be lied to, then don't lie to others. If you want others to keep their word to you, then you be a person of integrity and keep your word to others.

"Give, and it shall be given you; good measure, pressed down and shaken together, and running over, shall men give into your bosom. For with the same measure that ye mete withal it shall be measured to you again." Luke 6:38

"But be ye doers of the Word, and not hearers only, deceiving your own hearts. But whoso looketh into the perfect law of liberty and continueth therein, he being not a forgetful hearer, but a doer of the Word, this man shall be blessed in his deed." James 1:22 & 25

Withholding

Ask God for blessing and then withholding it from others hinders us from receiving it ourselves. 1 Peter 3:9 finishes up by saying that we are not to return insult for insult. Giving insults for some people is a national pastime. They seem to be invigorated by insult exchanges.

The same is true with cursing. If we give insults, we get insulted. Cursing people while in traffic for example, sets a measure where we will be more stalled in traffic. Or if we are asking for something evil to happen to someone and we rejoice when it does, then we should not be surprised when we are in difficult places.

> *"He who withholds grain, the people will curse him, but blessing will come on the head of he who sells it."*
> *Proverbs 11:26*

What's the idea here?

If I want blessing, I have to develop a lifestyle of blessing others. What we speak about others or to others is like a boomerang. It will come back!

> *"A faithful man shall abound with blessings; but he that maketh haste to be rich shall not be innocent."*
> *Proverbs 28:20*

Abounding is a picture of a reservoir or storage, and in many cases refers to water. We are created to be a reservoir of life sustaining encouragement. We will get deeper into this later.

Faith

A person who is full of faith will have the ability to bless continually. Why? Becoming a blesser is an issue of faith, because when we bless we are doing it through faith. Human nature is resistant to blessing others. This becomes more difficult when we come across people who continually take blessings and never give them. Oh, but how we love to hang around those who do bless! Thankfully, that natural tendency can be overcome by looking to our perfect example- JESUS CHRIST. He blessed the tax collectors and sinners who were looked down upon by society, and even children who were considered less important.

By being a blesser, Jesus, repelled every demonic force that came against Him on the cross. He refused to curse; instead, He blessed them. He was moving toward them in the opposite spirit.

Faith and Belief

"Faith comes from hearing and hearing by the Word of God." Romans 10:17

Faith and belief are not the same. Beliefs are formed from what we were trained and taught, and they create a foundation or a structure of values. Faith is the "now" and it comes by hearing. What we are hearing now produces faith, not what we heard 20 years ago, because that can wane with time. Faith is knowing inside our spirit at a particular moment God's desire and will for someone or something. We can then move to align ourselves with God's perspective. The knowing produces in us a readiness to speak the Lord's mind (His thoughts, His words) for that person or situation. We can know God's will for an individual or situation without being on our knees for 30 minutes! Though we do not know the specifics for the individual, we do know God's general will. The written Word becomes our reason for blessing. This eliminates being worried about whether we are doing it right, because we are

FAITH

following His example. Knowing God's revealed will creates confidence in prayer that God hears us.

"And all things, whatsoever ye shall ask in prayer, believing, ye shall receive them." Mathew 21:22

No wonder the book of Hebrews tells us that it is impossible to please God without faith (see Hebrews 11:6). Faith is agreement with God's perspective. Without question, seeing, someone's potential through the eyes of God makes it easier to bless. Faith is vital and essential to releasing the power of blessing. Faith is agreement with God's perspective.

I mentioned before that the more we choose to obey God and follow His perfect ways, we can be trusted by Him to hear and know His voice.

"And when He putteth forth His own sheep, He goeth before them, and the sheep follow Him, for they know His voice".
John 10: 4

A Word from Him

It was an ordinary day. I was going about my usual routine, praying throughout the day in the Spirit. I stopped because I felt urgency in my spirit to take the time to be still and be quiet before the Lord. I started to get a Word from Him in my mind. I was puzzled because I couldn't understand the reasoning behind what God was asking of me. In my natural mind it made no sense, but I knew His voice, so I obeyed.

FAITH

What God impressed in my spirit was to go to a nearby park and wait. There are several parks where I used to live, but I knew exactly which one He meant. Before I left, I asked Him to bless my obedience and the circumstances.

I have to say, I had no idea that I would be sitting there for as long as I did. It was at least an hour that I sat on a bench praying in the Spirit. I noticed when I first got there that a young woman had arrived about the same time that I had. I suddenly knew that I was to pray for her. Then she looked over at me and started walking towards me. We introduced ourselves and started talking. After a short getting acquainted kind of conversation, I told her that I believe in Jesus and that He had put on my heart to come to this park and pray.

She suddenly got very excited and told me that she had been having some problems and that she lived out of state, but had come to stay with some family to get away for a while. She said she stopped at the park just to think things out. I asked her if I could pray for her. She said yes, and the Lord gave me a word for her. She cried and hugged me. It so happened that it was a truth she wasn't quite ready for, but she received it because she had asked God for an answer and she knew it was the right thing to do. I asked God to bless her and her circumstances with His will in her life. We even kept in touch for a while.

I share this because again, the more we seek to obey God and walk in His ways, the more we can hear Him direct every step in our lives. Also, giving people a word of blessing

FAITH

is not always pleasant to the Adamic nature, but nevertheless, it's what God, our heavenly Father knows is best for us. We can bless others by speaking His truth in love, if we really love them as He does.

Don't ask me why, but because God is sovereign and He made each one of us, He alone knows what His will is for our lives. He chose to start teaching me about what I speak from a young age. I learned by experience that the results were sometimes good, sometimes bad, sometimes very good, and sometimes very bad.

As I spent more time in His Word and time in prayer, especially praying in the Spirit, I began to trace the times that a blessing came and also how fast or slow they came.

"And I, if I be lifted up from the earth, will draw all men unto Me." John 12:32

TIME TO PRAY

Father, I come and present myself before You as an instrument of blessing. I want to be an oracle, a mouthpiece to blessing. Lord, give me the vocabulary so that I turn away from being so quick to curse and speak evil (or contrary to Your will) of people, and instead bless them with Your will and Your perfect intentions in their life. Give me the words to bless those that I don't even know.

FAITH

I speak grace over my children. I see the situation not as insurmountable or destructive, but I see it with the eyes of grace. I see what can be. Lord, help me not to have a narrow mind and a mind so that I cannot hear You because I insist that You agree with what I think. Spirit of The Lord, help me right now. Bring me to a place of maturity, so that the power that works with me is not self-destructive, but one where I am proclaiming the blessing of others that I might be a blesser.

CHAPTER 4

THE BLESSING WE INHERIT

I have a friend, whose real name I will not use. I will call her Tricia. She was tied up in a dispute after dispute over a family inheritance. According to her, it was like "THE FAMILY FEUD". The large amount of land could not be sold because of the family's terrible disagreements among her siblings. The situation was a messy affair. The rivalry lasted for a long time.....way too long. The lawyers were not able to help in the disbursing of the settlement. No one had told her that receiving an inheritance would be this complicated.

Tricia and I are good friends, as well as sisters in the Lord. She would listen intently on the teaching about the blessing from God and what He will do when we apply His Word. She knew about the power of blessing. Obviously, her family needed it. Just as the truth about blessing was sinking in, God showed her a picture of a web that had been spun and was entangling her siblings. It was time to kill the spider of cursing and untangle its web from around her family's inheritance through blessing. So she began by considering what the Lord would speak over her family. She consistently blessed her rivaling siblings, even in the face of their resistance to God's intentions for their lives and children. In just a matter of a few days, the call came. They were ready to settle in an agreeable manner. Blessing took Tricia from months of heartache and pain to a resolution in a matter of days.

I have story after story of friends and family whose prayers have been answered. These people did not just hear about the power of blessing... they put it to practice. I have witnessed first hand the many changes in my friends' lives, as well as my own, as a direct result of blessing. The power of God in blessing is not a theory. I have seen it work and have invested in it. Now, more than ever, I am persuaded of the truth that God desires to bless man, but even more so, He desires for us to bless man.

My husband and I are from Ohio, but we now live in Florida. Living here is also a direct result of what I chose to speak. I have been saved (born again), for about 40 years, and I have learned to know the voice of my Savior.

"And when he putteth forth His own sheep, He goeth before them, and the sheep follow Him; for they know His voice. And a stranger will they not follow, but will flee from him; for they know not the voice of strangers." John 10:4,5

At one point while we were still living in Ohio, I heard the voice of the Lord in my spirit. Clearly, He said that we

THE BLESSING WE INHERIT

would be moving to Florida. There were many things that would have to take place before that could happen. Among them was convincing my husband. You see, he is a real Buckeye at heart. So I began to consistently speak God's blessing over this whole move....starting with my husband.

I went to God and asked Him to bless him with His will and intentions in this matter. I stood back and watched God move . He began to talk about moving to Florida, making phone calls, inquiring about housing, and a church, etc. It would also involve the sale of our house, which according to the realtor he called, wouldn't sell because of the "economy". I just smiled, and again, consistently kept speaking God's blessing over the sale of our house.

There are many other details involved in which I saw God's promise of blessing, but I share only these two details because it would take too long. Well, our house sold in three weeks to our neighbor, whom after the sale of the house was done, gave his heart to Jesus. Both my husband and I asked God to bless him with His salvation. We prayed with him and led him to the Lord. We have now lived in Florida for almost two years, and his wife has since then also been saved. We continue to speak the blessing over both of them and their family. Praise God, from whom all blessings flow!

God blesses us so that we can be a blessing. He blessed us with the sale of our house so that we in turn could be a blessing to our neighbor and his family. Isn't that what He said to Abraham?

THE BLESSING WE INHERIT

"Get out of your country, from your family, and from your Father's house, to a land that I will show you. I will make you a great nation; I will bless you and make your name great; and you shall be a blessing. I will bless those who bless you and curse those who curse you; and in you all the families of the earth shall be blessed." (Gen.12:1-3)

This is speaking to us, His children. The power of blessing is working inside us. When we don't bless, this power lays dormant. We just become recipients of blessing. We can have plenty of stuff, but we are not happy because we were designed by God to be blessers. Our greatest joy is when we are sowing the intentions of God. Any unhappiness with our body, marriages, children etc. is due to us not blessing them.

By blessing, we receive God's intended goodness toward us in full capacity, including long life and healthy relationships. We become partakers or partners of what and whom we are blessing. That act gives the Holy Spirit an even stronger leadership through our lives. It then becomes a lifestyle of obedience.

Understanding our calling to be blessers causes us to live more purposeful lives. Releasing blessing moves us closer to our intended destiny, and our lives will display patterns of fullness and success. By this, we further show the world God's generous heart. There are many more things that I am going to be telling you about. But, for now I would like to give you a prayer.

THE BLESSING WE INHERIT

"Father, I really want to bless and be a person of blessing. I want to walk in the power of your Spirit. I know the price for that, and it is not too difficult, nor is it far away. It is right in my mouth. Cause me Lord, to become a blesser in this city. Even as you said that you blessed Abraham so that he could become a blessing to all the families of the earth. Father, I ask that you would "touch my lips" as Isaiah said, with coals from off the altar, that I may become a mouthpiece and speak as a person called and sent from God to bless. Deliver me from evil and deliver me from cursing for Your name's sake, so that I might enter into the inheritance that You have already given to us."

CHAPTER 5

ACCORDING TO GOD

"For My thoughts are not your thoughts, neither are your ways My ways, saith the Lord. For My thoughts are higher, so are My ways higher than your ways, and My thoughts your thoughts." Isaiah 55:8,9

I felt it necessary to start off this next lesson with this verse because it will be very important to keep in your mind that God knows more, sees more, and is much more deep than we are.

I prayed about this chapter because I really had to ask God to help me convey His thoughts for this teaching to be developed. It is a real spiritual eye opener, and I still have to ask God for His power to reveal His thoughts in how blessing versus cursing according to Him. It saddens me to have known and to know even now, sincere Christians who truly believe that if someone sins against them, all they have to do is ask God to let something happen to them. Then perhaps they will learn their lesson and turn to Him. I have never found that to be true. God simply will not do that. There was a man who grew up hearing his mother pray for his father this way; "Lord, just dangle him over the flames and let him feel the heat of hell." And feel it he did, and so did his family. He knew about the teaching of speaking blessings and not curses over people, so one day he asked his mother, "why don't you pray the peace of God on him so we can get some peace ourselves?" Thank God, she finally did. His mom did not know it at the time, and neither do some Christians. Asking God to turn up the heat on someone so they will repent rarely works.

You see, this is what you really have to get ahold of.....are you ready? God defends the cursed under the new covenant. If you curse someone...He will defend them. This new covenant truth runs counter to what many are taught. If we curse someone, God will withstand us even if the one we cursed is not a good person. Cursing puts us in opposition to the reason Jesus came to die. (Galatians 3:13) Christ redeemed us from the curse of the law, having become a curse for us- for it is written, "Cursed is everyone who hangs on a tree." When we set a standard of cursing or speaking evil toward others, then God by His own nature and righteousness, will defend the one we cursed. We can then find ourselves opposing God. Isn't that interesting? If someone curses you, God will defend you even if He doesn't agree with what you are doing. I told you this would be deep. Remember His ways are higher than ours. God is a father, a father does not want other people to say bad things about their children or get on them for doing wrong. Now, the father of the child may want to get on them for doing wrong, but he doesn't want you to do it. As a parent, you will defend your children to the fullest degree. In the same manner, God will defend the cursed, even if it is against a sibling. I know you are probably shocked, and possibly in total disagreement with me, but proclaiming the good news is staking the claim of Jesus. He came to release people from their pain, and not to tell people how deep they are in sin.

"The Spirit of The Lord is upon Me, because He anointed Me to preach the gospel to the poor. He has sent Me to proclaim release to the captives, and recovery of sight to the blind, to set those free who are oppressed". Luke 4:18

I quote this verse to explain the meaning of the word proclaim here and what it means in this context. In this particular verse, it means to advance and claim a right to something, or to assert and demand the recognition of a right, title, or possession. So here proclaim means "to advance the claim".

In the previous verse, it means to proclaim God's goodness and mercy and favor in a situation. Blessing is proclaiming this truth and the intentions of God over our families and all that concern us. Jesus fulfilled (Luke 4:18). His life on earth was given to the preaching of the good news, healing and delivering the oppressed. He forgave sins. Even the sins of the woman who was caught in the act of adultery and deserved punishment according to the law, (John 8:3-5; 7-11). Forgiving her did not mean that Jesus was agreeing with her sin. Instead, He stopped the curse on her life by telling her to go and sin no more. Jesus's mission was to save the world, not condemn it. And with His life, He delivered humankind from the curse. It was a complete work and it was enough.

The prophet Amos wrote, *"can two walk together, unless they are agreed?"* (Amos 3:3 NKJV).

Being in agreement is vital for any relationship. Our idea of agreement is that we cannot agree if we do not feel the same way, but that is not God's way of agreement. He is on a higher level. Agreement with God is to say what He is saying. We do not have to feel the same way He does. Just because we feel the same way as someone, does not mean that we are in agreement. Are we being hypocrites then, if we are blessing someone when we want something bad to happen instead?
NO! We don't have to agree with what they are doing or with what we are blessing. We are simply agreeing with God. Feelings can change, but God's Word does not. Blessing is being in agreement with the Word of the Lord, and that truth remains regardless of feelings or situations. I have been in conversations where someone would say, "well, I think God should do this", and my reply was, "what does God's Word say?" It disarmed them, especially if they knew what God's Word says.

The point is this---what I think is not invalid, but agreeing with what God's Word is saying is more important. Agreeing with God is standing and declaring His will "on earth as it is in Heaven". That is being on His side.

ACCORDING TO GOD

"But the hour is coming, and now is, when the true worshipers will worship the Father in spirit and in truth; forThe Father is seeking such to worship Him." John 4:23 NKJV

The word worship is very similar to "blessing". Since God is seeking true worshippers, we can say that He is seeking blessers. God looks at how we treat others as a form of worshipping him. He seeks blessers who will bless the name of The Lord and those He created to worship Him. He is seeking people on earth to declare what He is expressing in Heaven.

WHAT IS A CURSE?

Man's fallen nature tends to oppose blessing. When questioned by God as to why he was hiding, Adam's first response was to blame Eve, which in actuality, he was blaming God for giving him a woman like her. Eve, in turn, blamed her sin on the devil (Gen. 3:9-13). Our very fallen nature is to blame others for our condition. You name it, we blame it. We refuse to accept the fact that when it's all said and done, we have been given a free will to choose our own actions, reactions, thoughts or decisions. How we speak, how we treat others, starting with our spouse and our children. Our attitude is our choice and no one else's.

"Therefore to him that knoweth to do good and doeth it not, to him it is sin." James 4:17

Once God has opened our eyes of understanding to His truth, and we know how He wants us to be, we can no longer blame anyone but ourselves.

"The way of a fool is right in his own eyes; but he that hearkeneth unto council is wise. We are either blessing or cursing; there is no neutral ground. God is the blesser and the devil is the cursor, or the "accuser of the brethren". Prov.12:15

"Then I heard a loud voice in heaven saying, "now the salvation, and the. power, and the Kingdom of our God and the authority of His Christ have come, for the accuser of the brethren has been thrown down. He who accuses them before our God day and night". Rev. 12:10

Curses are not just confined to speaking evil words over people. There are different ways people curse.

1.) Accusations are a curse

Most people do not want to commit sin. The reason why most people do is because they are under a curse and their eyes are blind. But it is possible for someone under constant accusations to come to a place where they begin to agree with accusations. Agreement with accusations is a yield sign for sin. I have had people say to me that since they were accused of something all their life, they might as well do it. By agreeing and operating under the accusations, they in turn begin to accuse others, and a curse becomes part of their lives.

2.) Withholding God's heart and intention for someone is also a curse.

Someone's negative actions or attitude toward us is not even an excuse (no matter how justified we feel about it) to deny them blessing.

You see, we can take on their spirit by withholding any affection, blessing, or love which is due them. So, when a husband withholds blessings from his wife, his prayers can literally be hindered.

"Husbands, likewise dwell with them with understanding, giving honor to the wife, as to the weaker vessel, and as being heirs together of the grace of life, that your prayers may not be hindered." Peter 3:7 NKJV

This does not mean that a woman has permission to use that as a scripture against her husband. God places great value in our treatment and attitude toward each other-- especially those in our own household.

3.) It is also a curse to speak anything contrary to God's will or intention over someone.

After all, it is our opinion against God's.

"Every way of a man is right in his own eyes; but The Lord pondereth the hearts." Prov.21:2

So to say that someone will not amount to anything or to recount their failures are acts that fall into the cursing category.

We may pride ourselves for having an opinion about everything, but this habit brings us in agreement with the accuser. Being opinionated is a difficult habit to quit. You see, it is possible to live a mediocre life while cursing people. However, the life of joy and blessing comes from those who bless with the right thoughts, words and actions toward others. Cursing reveals the heart is full of bitterness and resentment which will flow out of the mouth. We may never call for divination on anyone, but we can certainly curse them with these kinds of words and attitudes.

The truth of the matter is cursing affects us more than the one we may be cursing. Unfortunately, the fallen nature of man is to curse or speak evil, in a mean tone or harshly against those who did something to us. Have you ever heard anyone say, "I can tell them off in a heartbeat"? We may walk away feeling good and think, "Boy, I sure told them off", but at that moment they have entered into agreement with the cursing. We may win a battle of words but loose the entire war of living in the favor of the Lord.

" Who is wise, and he shall understand these things? prudent, and he shall know them? for the ways of The Lord are right, and the just shall walk in them: but the transgressors shall fall therein." Hosea 14:9

CHAPTER FIVE - Part Two

(Prov. 26:2) Curses cannot land without a cause. The blood of Jesus is our covering from them. Still, there are some things that can open the door to a curse. Fear is one. It can empower a curse. Severe emotional wounding is another; like wounds from extreme violations such as molestation, rape, and incest. Agreeing with accusations and having faith in them are also invitations to a curse. By mulling over our lies, we can literally receive them into our spirits and allow a curse to take root. Curses spread just like rumors-- by someone agreeing and b lessing that lie. Those who indulge in cursing have built a landing pad for curses to alight and build strongholds.

Despising prophetic utterances is another avenue for curses. Sometimes a prophetic word may sound like condemnation, but if given in love, it is a blessing where there is a need for enlightenment. This path is so often overlooked. I operate in a prophetic anointing, but I do not prophesy just so I can say, "look at me". I am gifted in the prophetic! True prophecy is all about blessing people. I am very aware of the responsibility of the prophetic gift. For us to despise prophetic blessing as Esau despised his birthright, is to despise the blessing of the Lord. I am not referring to so called prophecy that does not edify or speak of the heart of Christ for His bride. When we curse others, we line ourselves up with the accuser. Sometimes that manifests itself in difficulties in our relationships and an overall lack of favor upon our lives.

Constantly feeling rejected or being easily offended

can also be a sign of habitual cursing flowing through us. We might be cursing a spouse, child,, boss or person in authority, for example. For many of us, we assume God feels the same way we do. We like to believe that God thinks the way we think. If we don't like it, then He must not like it. Joshua, Moses' successor, had the same perspective.

"Now it came to pass about when Jesus was by Jericho, that he lifted up his eyes and looked, and behold, a man was standing opposite him with his sword drawn in his hand, and Joshua went to him and said to him, 'are you for us or for our adversaries'? He said, '"Neither, rather I indeed come now as captain of the host of the Lord." Joshua 5:13-14

Joshua wanted to know which side the angel's sword would stand with. The angel said that he was with neither, but he was on the Lord's side, which stands for righteousness and the blessing of the Lord. Let's pause here for a moment. There is also something else I would like for you to see here about angels.

"Are they not all ministering spirits, sent forth to minister for them who shall be heirs of salvation"? Hebrews 1:14

What I want to point out here is that we Christians look at this verse, and go around charging the angels to minister to us, (which they will do), but according to the previous verse in Josh.5:14 they will only obey what God says. So, if we are cursing someone or speaking to or of someone contrary to God's will and purpose for them, then even the angels will not move to minister to us. But when we line ourselves up by speaking in agreement with His word and His intentions, they will proceed to minister to us. And what God wants is for us to bless others with His will for that individual or circumstance.

Blessing is not about sides. This is not to say that we should neglect positions of righteousness, but even at times where people are clearly in the wrong, we can still bless them. Blessing is about seeing what God intends to happen, not the way it is at the moment. Don't get caught up in hostility or an arguing spirit.

Sometimes we have to ask ourselves, why am I reacting with such hostility? Why am I really angry? Is it because what he or she said to me is right and in agreement with God? Is it because in my pride I want them to agree with me so I can feel better? Do I humbly and truthfully want the blessing that this truth will bring me, which is deliverance from the selfish nature of Adam? Will I choose to be thankful, swallow my pride and be blessed because my wife, pastor, or friend cares enough to help me see where I have been blind?

Wow, thats a hard pill to swallow isn't it? That's not quite what I have heard before of how to prepare myself for blessing, but nevertheless, this is why pride is one of the things that God hates. It gets in His way to bring us the blessing! Blessing doesn't always come with a good feeling, but it does tell us how mature we are or not. That person might knowingly have chosen to risk friendship and relationship with you, and cared enough about you to tell you what others will not.

Before reacting with anger, go and take some time with God, and ask Him to bless you with a change of attitude, and the blessing of deliverance, so that you can learn to communicate with people even if they don't feel the same way you do. After all, you just might not be in agreement with God's Word and someone cares enough not to leave you there to continue cursing, when you thought you were blessing.

Division is exactly what satan wants. Blessing breaches division, even if it causes us to become humble, (that's a word our flesh doesn't like). The blessing of God's truth injects the spirit of Christ into the situation. Resist being pulled into arguing spirits. The media loves to do this. They spew out cursing, much to the devil's delight. Instead let a prophetic heart show what God would really intend for the situation. When our eyes are on Jesus, we can intercede and bless whoever is in authority in a nation. We want to answer the call to pray and bless. In this way, we can resist the spirit of confusion that has come upon the nation and the church.

The devil always wants us to take sides. We may see people that disagree with us and we begin to complain or act self-righteous. "Lord, they are out there prophesying; they are not part of us". "They don't believe the same way we do." This is the same thing that Moses faced. Numbers 11 tells us about two men named Eldad and Medad, who were prophesying among the camp of Israel. Joshua, a young man at that time, suggested to Moses that he restrain them because they were not part of their recognized group. Moses in his wisdom, replied to Joshua, "Are you jealous for my sake?" He said, "Would that all the Lord's people were prophets..". (Num.11:29). What a wonderful sight to behold if all of God's people would bless those they had contact with!

Pressures to take sides in matters do come. I've had my fair share of them. Situations have happened in my life where I was literally accused of not being a "Christian" because I didn't choose to side with someone to "keep the peace". I have been accused of causing trouble instead. How could I be their friend and not be on their side, cursing their offender! My refusal only stirred their anger.

Whose side was I on anyway? As a follower of Christ, I am not to choose your side, or their side, just so I will be liked. I am to be on God's side. Friends or family may want you on their side, but a friend of God stands on the side of God. As your friend, you need me to be blessing. You in a gentle, tactful and honest way, and not just on how to be on your side. It is possible to be on the wrong side. One thing I do know is that the only side God favors is the side where we are committed to blessing with God's will and intentions.

People sometimes become angry with God because of unanswered prayers or unfulfilled hopes. It never occurs to them that God may have desired to do it, but cursing has held up the answers they have waited for. Remember, (1st Peter 3:7), which exhorts husbands and wives to live in such a way that their prayers are not hindered. God does hear from friends and family that we were to prepare ourselves for the hardest time of parenting.

I know now that God was teaching me even then not to accept their words. I would speak out, "NO, they will be fine and they are not going to give us a hard time at all". I didn't realize then, that I was agreeing with God's will for them. I said they will grow up to serve the Lord. Now don't get me wrong, they were not perfect and neither were we perfect parents, but we taught them the importance of being in church, listening to and obeying God's Word, and we continued through the years to speak God's will and intention over each of them. We continued to bless them with His will and not the words of man.

They are all grown now. The two oldest are in their 40's, and the two youngest are in their 30's. None of them ever gave us a hard time. They are all married and our son's wives are both born again and our daughter's husbands are also. We have ten grandchildren who are being brought up in church. The ones that have reached the age of accountability are all saved, and the youngest are being raised to know the Lord. Of course, a little sprinkling of good old fashioned spankings, (which were few) also helped as well as living the life in front of them with the revealed knowledge of God that we had.

As I look back, I see where without having the teaching from the Bible about speaking the blessing, God was already preparing me to one day teach about this wonderful key to be blessed as we travel on this earth. He put in our hearts to bless our children, our finances, and to bless others. He taught us not to accept anything that was not spoken in line with His word. He taught us to keep our focus on Him and what He says. He is not a respecter of persons. He will do the same for you.

TIME TO PRAY

Father, I come and present myself before You as an instrument of blessing. I want to be an oracle, a mouth piece to blessing. Lord, give me the vocabulary so that I turn away from being so quick to curse and speak evil (or contrary to Your will) of people, and instead bless them with Your will and Your perfect intentions in their life. Give me the words to bless those that I don't even know. I speak grace over my children. I see the situation not as insurmountable or destructive, but I see it with the eyes of grace. I see what can be. Lord, help me not to have a narrow mind and a mind so that I cannot hear You because I insist that You agree with what I think. Spirit of the Lord, help me right now. Bring me to a place of maturity, so that the power that works within me is not self-destructive, but one where I am proclaiming the blessing of others so that I might be a blesser.

CHAPTER 6

DO IT GOD'S WAY

I grew up in a very small town in Ohio. I have always told people that it is the real "Mayberry" of the old Andy Griffith show. Yes, everybody knows everybody and everyone's children grew up together and eventually married your friends' children. There were some exceptions. Those who actually dared to marry someone from another town or state. It's funny now as I look back it is almost unreal in this modern age that we live in to think that a place like that could actually exist. Why am I telling you this? Well, I need for you to understand that when a certain type of "business" opened up in our simple, old fashioned, safe little town, it was a shock to the majority of our townspeople that our city officials allowed it to open. Little did I know that God was going to someday use it as a part of my lesson of blessing and cursing.

In case you didn't guess, it was a topless nightclub. None of us in our church liked it, but there didn't seem to be anything we could do about it. In fact, my husband and I drove past it every time we went to church. There was a certain young man that attended our church. He was a very zealous young man in his faith in Christ, and he was determined that he was going to do something about it. Well, he gathered a few other Christian brothers together and went there and picketed, cursed it, and everything else that they could do within the law. They went to the city officials and demanded that they close it down; God was on their side after all. Did God not hate idolatry, fornication, and who knows what else went on in there? Feeling assured that he was right on target, he went on his way for that day. Tomorrow he would be back to do it all over again. But, the next day, it was still there. Customers were streaming in and out, and it looked like there were more patrons than the last time. It could not be! How could it be flourishing when God was so against it? It seemed the more he cursed it, the more it flourished. I know he meant well, but in spite of doing all of those things, they never closed it down. This was quite a few years ago and as far as I know, it is still open.

Well, I have learned since then how much easier it would have been for them if he had applied a blessing instead of cursing them. God has allowed me to witness an almost identical situation in another state where the blessing was applied and resulted in a much different way. After many years went by, I heard about a pastor who also believes in the power of the tongue. I couldn't believe it when I heard his testimony. I believe that God allowed me to witness two very similar situations where God's way versus man's way were applied. It seems that there was also a young man with the same situation. He, too, cursed the place he was against... believing that he was pleasing God by wanting to get this place closed down. One day while on his faithful tour to curse the night club, the Lord brought to his remembrance what his pastor had been teaching about speaking the blessing. God spoke deep inside his heart. The Lord asked him, "why are you cursing the people that I have given my life for-- the same life that I gave for you?" Then the young man realized that the business was not the issue, but it was the blindness of those who patronized the place.

"But I say to you, love your enemies, bless those that curse you and pray for those who spitefully use you and persecute you." Mathew 5:44 NKJV

Bless his enemies? What a concept! Blessing apparently was God's way. God was "the God of the turn and return". This was new, but this was God's reply. Like someone learning a new language, he began to bless the owner of the club and the people inside. At first it was awkward, but he felt the pleasure of the Lord while blessing them. He realized that it was the goodness of the Lord that brings people to repentance (change). Within two weeks, the once thriving club had shut their doors without any notice. Cursing causes darkness to thrive, and blessing turns things for righteousness sake. What he learned is a lesson that many Christians never seem to grasp. Blessing is an attribute of God. This took the weight off his shoulders and the burden of having to punish his foes. A new strategy for spiritual warfare was opened to him.

"For the weapons of our warfare are not carnal, but mighty through God to the pulling down of strongholds. Casting down imaginations, and every high thing that exalted itself against the knowledge of God, and bringing into captivity every thought to the obedience of Christ. And having in a readiness to revenge all disobedience, when your obedience is fulfilled. Do ye look on things after the outward appearance? If any man trust to himself that he is Christ's, even so are ye Christ's. For though I should boast somewhat more of our authority, which the Lord hath given us for edification, and not for your destruction, I should not be ashamed." 2 Cor. 10: 4-8

God's plan for those who were caught up in frequenting that night club was not just for them to stop going, but for them to find Him as a greater joy than the pleasures of sin.

Many people can be convinced not to sin and still not find the place of enjoying their salvation from captivity. This is our challenge. For this is where many of us have failed and fallen into condemnation. Our tongue-- our vehicle for speech-- has taken many of us down the wrong path, but it is the one thing that we need for the release of the blessing. Thinking blessing is only the beginning. Blessing means to say something good and to empower. Speaking releases the blessing, and that calls our tongue into action. That also places a great responsibility on our tongue. We are literally prophesying or "breathing out" the breath of God as we bless.

Think about it. That is something not to be taken lightly. "Breathing out" blessing releases God's power to work in a person and situation. The words are there. The tongue waits. Soaking in eager anticipation of whatever the thoughts we let loose; it wags them to life. I know that sounds funny, but it's true. How awesome it is when the words are those that breath out the life of God! God has given us the wonderful gift of a free will, and so it is up to us to choose what we allow our tongue to confess. What power God has given us!

"Death and life are in the power of the tongue, and those who love it will eat its fruit." Proverbs 18:21

But not every tongue blesses. God has granted our tongue the power to wreak havoc or give life. Every day our mouths exercise that privilege. When the tongue has done its part, the rest of the body has to deal with the consequences of those words-- whether they were life giving or not. We may unknowingly be feasting on the tongue's sweet fruit or rotten yields, because what we have in a power packed appendage that is unruly. Add to that "a restless evil and full of deadly poison" and we are left with a body part that needs to be controlled.

"But the tongue can no man tame; it is an unruly evil, full of deadly poison". Honestly, no one wants something that powerful and toxic to be running loose." James: 3:8

We can name our tongue as the culprit, but in actuality, it is an unrenewed mind or heart that feeds the tongue its content. However, no one can tame the tongue (James 3:8). We have tried. So now what? Bridle it. Yes, like we do a horse. A horse is a large animal that can be trained and directed by having control of the bits and bridle placed over the tongue and head of the horse.

"Behold, we put bits in the horses' mouths, that they may obey us; and we turn about their whole body." James 3:3

James, a Son of thunder, and a man whose sharp tongue earned him an unforgettable place in the gospels-- knew what he was talking about.

"And when His disciples James and John saw this, they said, "Lord, wilt thou that we command fire to come down from Heaven and consume them, even as Elias did"? Luke 9:54

His tongue (and most of us can relate) was quick to condemn and bring judgment on any who disagreed with them at any given moment. James paints a good picture for us to understand the power of the tongue.

"Look at the ships also, they are so great and are driven by strong winds, are still directed by a very small rudder. Wherever the inclination of the pilot desires. So also the tongue is a small part of the body, and yet it boasts of great things. See how great a forest is set aflame by such a small fire." James 3:4-5

Get the picture? This small appendage can set a direction

and destiny just as a rudder directs a ship. We know that we cannot do this in our own strength. So where do we go?

"I will lift up mine eyes to the hills, from where cometh my help. My help cometh from the Lord, which made heaven and earth." Psalms 121:1-2

Here comes our help.... God's Holy Spirit is our coach who teaches us what to say.

"But the Comforter, which is The Holy Ghost, whom the Father will send in My name; He shall teach you all things and bring all things to your remembrance, whatever I have said unto you." John14:26

He is about truth, the truth that pertains to Jesus; and He is our hope for a bridled tongue.

"Howbeit when He, the Spirit of Truth is come, He will guide you into all truth; for He shall not speak of Himself, but whatsoever He shall hear, that shall He speak; and He will show you things to come." James 16:13

Bridling our tongue with a gentleness and vigilance beyond human ability. The Holy Spirit guides our tongue so it releases life more than death.

"For he that will love life, and see good days, let him refrain his tongue from evil, and his lips that they speak no guile; no thought or word escapes His patrol." I Peter 3:10

DO IT GOD'S WAY

Flagging the bad and releasing the good words that bless, begin to replace words that curse. Under His command, our tongue does not short-circuit our movement in the right direction. In the long run, bridling our tongue under the power of the Holy Spirit has one outcome-- Perfection. Definitely, the direction we should be moving towards. No matter what other people say, we can choose to keep our tongue under God's control. A tongue under control means a body and emotions are under control, too. Now that is priceless!

Being seasoned in the things of God does not excuse us from keeping our tongue under the Holy Spirits' control. The prophet Isaiah recognized this truth. Bathed in the Shekinah glory of God--- the breathtaking and Holy presence of the Lord--- He was only aware of one thing; the unacceptable condition of his mouth, especially for one who spoke for God.

"Woe is me, for I am ruined! Because I am a man of unclean lips, and I live among a people of unclean lips; for my eyes have seen the King, the Lord of hosts." Isaiah 6:5

He was a man sold out to God. His speech needed to reflect that commitment. Forget how he may stand out among the people; he wanted nothing else than to speak forth the will and love of the God whose splendor he was permitted to see. He cried out for God to deal with his unruly mouth. And God did, with a burning hot coal.

"Then flew one of the seraphims unto me, having a live coal in his hand, which he had taken with the tongs from off the altar. And he laid it upon my mouth and said, 'Lo, this hath touched thy lips; and thine iniquity is taken away, and thy sin purged." Isaiah 6:6,7

Maturity is more than just living long enough to know the consequences of our good or bad choices. Nor is it doing everything perfectly, but instead, it is allowing the Holy Spirit to direct our tongues in the way we need to go. Our words and lifestyle will reflect that inward movement. We learn to breathe out His words and life, and abandon the desire to speak against our God-given destiny. No matter how big or small it may be.

CHAPTER 7

THE AARONIC BLESSING

What did the Jewish Patriarchs know about the mystery of imparting the blessing? Most people don't realize this, but the early church was founded on the Aaronic Blessing. This blessing is found in Numbers 6:22-27

"And the Lord spake unto Moses, saying: Speak unto Aaron and unto his sons, saying, this is the way ye shall bless the children of Israel, saying unto them, The Lord bless thee, and keep thee: The Lord make His face shine upon thee, and be gracious to thee: The Lord lift up His countenance upon thee, and give thee peace. And they shall put My name upon the children of Israel; and I will bless them."

It is so important that you understand the revelation that's been hijacked from the church of this ancient blessing. I believe that God is restoring it to the church.

God gave Moses the greatest challenge that man has

ever had in pastoring people. He had several million people counting the children and the wives, and they had a slavery mentality; no self-esteem and no self-worth. He gave them three pillars of faith to change their lives into a great viable nation, to respect and honor themselves. Those same three pillars of faith can be used to transform a person with no self-esteem and no self-worth. The first was the blood covenant. We call it Passover. The second was the moral code. We call it the Ten Commandments. God gave them to him on Mount Siani. However, the one that releases the favor of God upon the people was what we call the High Priestly blessing, found in Numbers 6: 22-27, which I previously quoted, and it is called the Aaronic Blessing. God gave it to Moses, and He commanded him to have Aaron and his sons speak that blessing over His people every time they gathered together.

Look at the very last line of the 27th verse. Read it slowly and meditate on it for a minute. Did you get the impact of it? God says, HE HIMSELF, would be present when the blessing is spoken and that His name would be placed upon the people, and that HE would do the blessing. We are His vessels. It is not me, and it is not you that fulfills the words of blessing spoken, IT IS GOD HIMSELF!

"So shall My Word be that goeth forth out of My mouth: it shall not return unto me void, but it shall accomplish that which I please, and it shall prosper in the thing whereto I send it." Isaiah 55:11

This is why when we bless someone or a circumstance

with His Word, His will, and His intentions, it is accomplished.

God's Word is life, and He keeps His Word. All that we have to do is release it with our tongue, and we don't have to wait for a "feeling". He just wants us to do our part by being a blesser. God has shown me through the years to bless those that curse me. He said, "If you do, I'll open up doors for you that no man can close, and I'll put a hedge of protection around you". He is ready to do the same for you and all His children.

"Whoso keepeth his mouth and his tongue keepeth his soul from troubles." Proverbs 21:23

When we speak a word for good or bad, that word goes out to perform the thing we spoke. Every word that we speak has behind it a blessing or a curse. We are caught in a snare by the words of our mouths. (Proverbs 18:7) "A fool's mouth is his destruction, and his lips are the snare of his soul". Our confession can defeat us, because the words that we speak have a spirit behind them. We are today what our confession was yesterday.

We Are What We Say

In times past, I have been through great pessimism, and a time of great fear; the fear of man and the fear of failure. I was so easily discouraged. Then I realized why, as I took inventory of my own words. "I can't do that"; "I suffer from

THE AARONIC BLESSING

migraines"; "I feel depressed"; "I'm so discouraged"; "they are mean"; "she lies to me all the time"; "I'm annoyed"; "I'm frustrated"; "I'm lonely"; "I'm sad"; "I'm so nervous"; "I'm angry"; "I'm not as smart as she is"; etc. and etc. My words were loaded with poison. The words that I spoke created a spirit and an atmosphere. They ministered either life or death to me.

When I don't feel well, I can say one of two things, "I just don't feel well today" or I can declare (Isaiah 53:5) "By His stripes I am healed", and continue to keep speaking His Word and believe for the manifestation of my healing.

I can say, "I don't like her" or I can say (Romans 5:5) "The love of God is shed abroad in my heart by the Holy Ghost". If we speak a thing long enough, our spiritual ears will hear it, and then it becomes a feeling. If we speak it long enough we will have it!

Saul said, "I can't do it". God said that there isn't any need to try. David's brother said, "We can't do it". God said they couldn't. David ran out and said, "I can do it". God said that David can do it, and he slew the invincible Goliath.

Joshua and Caleb said, "we are well able to do it", and God said they were going to possess the land. As we speak, so shall it be. If we say "We can't pay our bills this month", God says, "they can't pay their bills". But if we confess, "God will supply all of our needs". (Phil. 4:19) "But my God shall supply all my needs according to His riches in glory by

Christ Jesus". Then God says, "It's on the way". You can say, "I can't afford it". Someone else says, "My Father is rich in houses and lands". (Psalms 50:10) "For every beast of the forest is Mine, and the cattle upon a thousand hills". God says, "They've got it". I can say, "we don't have any food because of the economy", or I can say (Psalms 50:12) "If I were hungry, I would not tell thee:(speak it) for the world is mine, and the fullness thereof". I know these are many examples, but I really want you to understand how to live a lifestyle of agreement with His Word.

God's Vocabulary:

As we speak the promises of God, those promises become ours. For example:

"This book of the law, shall not depart out of thy mouth; but thou shalt meditate therein day and night, that thou mayest observe to do according to all that is written therein: for then thou shalt make thy way prosperous, and then thou shalt have good success." Joshua 1:8

God wanted Joshua to continually speak the word of God and claim God's promises. He told Joshua, "I want My word to be in you. Never let My words stop going out of your mouth. Keep repeating the promises. Keep speaking My Word and meditate on it."

When the Word of God has become a part of us, we will think like God thinks and talk like God talks. Just like a child that repeats his parent's words until he has the same vocabulary. God said, if My Word is in your mouth and you have meditated on it, then you are going to be full of faith and full of power and full of victory! Jesus said, "My words are spirit and they are life". He never spoke one word of discouragement in His life. He never said one thing that was pessimistic or full of unbelief. Jesus never once doubted the promises of God. He never spoke out a word that would bring anything but life.

When we speak in line with God's Word out loud...we speak our way right into glory and into victory--- right into faith and power--- right into health and life--- right on up and out of defeat and despair! We are going to start speaking over others and ourselves the blessing of deliverance and health and wholeness and prosperity because it is the will of God. But, we (you and I) must speak it.

Jesus related to people on the basis of the potential He saw in their lives. He called His unregenerated, untrained disciples the " salt of the earth " and the " light of the world " (Mathew 5:13-14).

He saw what they would become through the word He spoke to them daily. When Jesus told Peter that he would deny Him three times, He prefaced it with the words " when thou art converted, strengthen thy brothers " (Luke 22: 32). He could have said, (if you are converted)... but, He said when. He could have told his disciples that if they stayed with Him long enough and tried hard they might become the salt of the earth and the light of the world.

THE AARONIC BLESSING

But Jesus was able to see the possibilities in His disciples. So, He called them " salt " and " light ". They were already that in the heart of Jesus, so they became what He spoke over them. (Romans 4:17) As it is written, I have made thee a father of many nations, before him who believed, even God, who quickeneth the dead, and calleth those things which be not as though they were. He declared a thing and watched it be established.

When I was a little girl, I had a friend who never received blessings from her parents; they were concerned parents who took her to church every Sunday to help her learn to live the good life. They were critical of every mistake she made and warned her that if she didn't change her ways she would turn out to be a failure in life. Debby (not her real name) became nearly everything her parents warned her she would become. They could never seem to see beyond Debby's immediate attitude or behavior. Their attitude toward her was controlled by Debby's actions, not their faith.

It was by faith that the patriarchs spoke blessings over their children. They blessed from the heart, expecting all that they said over their children to come to pass.

Parents should pray, asking God to give them the ability to visualize the successful future of their children. With a clear vision of the potential in each child, the blessing can be spoken with authority and confidence. Since all discipline should be designed to produce good character, correction can be given within the context of blessing. If the parents do not believe in the future of their children, the children's lives will be one up hill- battle after another.

Let me add this. If you have children who are grown and are not serving God, you can still start speaking blessings over them now. Remember the story of the woman in (Mathew15: 22-28).

"And behold a woman of Canaan came out of the same coasts, and cried unto Him, saying, Have mercy on me, O Lord, thou son of David; my daughter is grievously vexed with a devil. But He answered her not a word. And His disciples came and besought Him, saying, Send her away; for she crieth after us. But He answered and said. I am not sent but unto the lost sheep of the house of Israel. Then came she and worshiped Him, saying, Lord, help me. But He answered and said, it is not meet to take the children's bread, and to cast it to dogs. And she said, truth, Lord; yet the dogs eat of the crumbs, which fall from their master's table. Then Jesus answered and said unto her, O woman great is thy faith; be it unto thee even as thou wilt. And her daughter was made whole from that very hour."

In verse 23- it says " but He answered her (spoke) not a word. Then in verse 28- Jesus answered and said (spoke). That because of her faith, her daughter was made whole. You too can send the word of God and speak His blessing over them and they will be healed; physically, mentally, emotionally, financially, spiritually, or whatever it might be. God's Word is never too late and there is no distance that His word cannot be sent to. He is faithful and true, His Word never returns void and accomplishes what it is sent out to perform. And He is always on time. So don't be discouraged. Don't let the enemy lie to you and tell you that it's too late. As long as you have the "breath of life- His Word" in you, then you can still speak His Word, His breath of life over them. And remember...it is Him, not you that is doing the " blessing". With Him all things are possible when you line yourself up with His Word. You can still start now to speak God's word of blessing over every relationship you are in. Your marriage, children, family, friends, whatever circumstance etc. We serve " The Great I Am" the God of the now.

Isaac asked Esau to hunt game and prepare his favorite dish so that he could eat it before speaking the blessing.

Having the right attitude is important to imparting the blessing to your children. Just as discipline cannot be conducted out of a heart of anger, blessing cannot come out of a critical attitude. David said, " Because of the house of the Lord our God I will seek thy good," (Psalms 122:9)

Parents should work through their own feelings before they attempt to bless. Once they reach the point that they " seek " the " good " for their children, they can begin to bless. That attitude can sometimes be achieved through prayer, or the study of the Holy Scriptures. If your children are grown and the devil is telling you that you messed up and it's too late. Call him what he is " a liar ". You don't have to stand for hours rebuking him. Simply go to our Heavenly Father, ask

THE AARONIC BLESSING

Him to forgive you with a truly repented heart. In some cases you may want to go to your children and ask them to forgive you. This goes for a spouse or anyone you may have cursed in the past. But if that is not possible, start speaking blessings over them now.

Every blessing in the bible is a verbal one.

"And God blessed them (Adam and Eve) and God said unto them..." David said, " for the sake of my brothers and my friends, I will now say, " My peace be within you ."
Genesis. 1:28 and Psalm 122:8

The blessing is always a spoken one. Not just a desire hidden in the heart of a parent. Words have power when they are released. Loving parents should find it easy to choose effective words to impart blessings to their children.

Laying on of Hands

Joseph drew his two young sons very close to his father, Jacob, so that he could lay his hands on the boys. *Genesis 18:13.* Mark 10:16 says that Jesus " took them (children) up in His arms, put His hands upon them, and blessed them."

The church has been faithful to practice the laying on of hands for the ordination of church leaders. In some cases, churches have preserved the work of healing through the laying on of hands. Yet few have taught the parents of the church to lay hands on their children and bless them. The rite

THE AARONIC BLESSING

is observed in many Jewish homes each Sabbath.

Children should be taught to kneel before their parents in expectation as they lay their hands upon their heads and impart blessing to them. As the hands come to rest upon the children, they will learn to expect God to impart special favor to them.

Paul said in Romans 11:29 that " the gifts and calling of God are without repentance. " That is, they are irrevocable. The permanency of the blessing spoken in faith gives strength to the children when they receive it. Isaac confirmed that the blessing, once given, had permanent value in the life of the one who received it. When Esau returned from hunting game and preparing his father's favorite dish, he and his father, Isaac, learned that someone else had already received the firstborn blessing. Upon hearing it, the text says, " Isaac trembled very exceedingly ". After inquiring as to whom it was that he had blessed, Isaac said almost abruptly, " yea, and he shall be blessed..." (Gen. 27:3). Blessings have great authority in the lives of the children who will receive them. And no one can take their blessings away if they respect them enough to keep them.

How Mature Are We?

Jesus instructed His disciples saying:

"love your enemies, bless them that curse you, do good to them that hate you, and pray for them, which despitefully use

you and persecute you. That ye may be the children of your Father which is in heaven; for He maketh the sun to rise on the evil and on the good, and sendeth rain on the just and the unjust." Mathew 5: 44-45

The command to love your enemy and bless those who curse you would be difficult to accept if one did not understand the meaning of verse 45. "That ye may be the children of your Father..." The word, children, in this passage is actually a word, which describes a mature son. A partner with his father. A better translation would be "sons". An immature, childish Christian would have difficulty with jealously and envy if the sun and rain soaked the crops of his neighbor who was an unbeliever. He would complain to God that he was not fair with him. After all, I serve You and You bless that unbeliever just as much as You do me, he would protest.

But the mature Christian does not judge God's love by the way He treats other people. He sees himself as a partner with God, having access to all the blessings of his heavenly Father. His point of reference is always the Lord, not others. His desire is like that of his Father in heaven. That makes him "perfect" or "mature", just as his Father is perfect. It is from God's viewpoint that the Christian is able to bless those who curse him. Paul emphasizes that point in 1 Cor. 4:12 when he says, Being reviled, we bless; being persecuted, we suffer it.

"And all the people departed every man to his house; and David returned to bless his house." 1 Chronicles 16:43

THE AARONIC BLESSING

We have seen in this lesson the principles upon which the blessing is established in the Word of God. I have devoted this chapter mainly to the blessing of our children because they are the future of the church. There is an old Jewish custom, which helps train children to show respect and reverence for the Word of God. Children, who develop a love for the Word and then receive the Word spoken over them in the form of blessing, enjoy spiritual benefits, which do not come to everyone.

Jewish parents will take a dip of honey and place it on the lips of their small children. As their babies savor the sweet taste of the honey, the parents tell them that the Word of God (Torah) is as sweet as honey and much to be desired. Jewish parents who observe that custom instill in their children a deep love and respect for the Torah, which makes it easy for them to receive their blessings.

Parents should be encouraged by the fact that the Lord is the one who blesses when they invoke His name over their children. Children who receive blessings from their parents on a regular basis will notice the difference in their lives. It will not be long until they will ask to be blessed if the parents overlook the responsibility.

"Train up a child in the way he should go; and when he is old, he will not depart from it." Prov. 22:6

You bless them by laying your hand on their heads and speaking God's Word over them. By daily speaking positive, encouraging, and edifying words over them. Let your children hear and see God's love in you, and they will develop a heartfelt hunger for Him and His Word.

CHAPTER 8

WHICH ONE ARE YOU?

Place a blesser and a curser in a difficult spot and there is a stark difference between their responses. Worshiping God and blessing Him with song after being beaten and thrown in prison is the farthest thing from a curser's mind. The "high praises of God" are not in their mouth, and they may be wishing for a "two edged sword in their hands" to whack off a few ears. But not blessers like Paul and Silas! (Acts: 16:22-34) Their hearts and mouths were set to bless God no matter their situation. Though it seemed natural to accuse God of allowing them to go through hardship, they chose to sing. The Lord heard their music and He dealt with their oppressors. Their songs became the key to the prison doors, and the opening for the jailer and his whole household to receive salvation. Wow! Paul and Silas could have missed that opportunity if they were busy whining and focusing on their troubles.

Even when an accuser appears to be blessing, the motive for it might be off the mark. Personal gain (if I bless, what's in it for me?) and comfort are generally in the forefront. Blessing to please others, and the fear of doing what pleases man because we might be rejected or not liked, is another motive that hinders us from God blessing us. We should have the heart of David. He wanted only to please God.

"Search me, O God, and know my heart; try me, and know my thoughts. And see if there be any wicked way in me, and lead me in the way everlasting." Psalms 139: 23-24

When Jesus rode into Jerusalem on the donkey, those people shouting "Hosanna" were literally saying, "Come and take your seat and rule Jerusalem". But God was not interested in Jesus kicking out the Roman occupation. Rather, the Roman conquerors were going to crucify Jesus. Even before Jesus was the bigger purpose; the redemption of the whole world. The only way to accomplish that was through His death. God wanted to rule in a higher place; the hearts of people. Not on some earthly throne! For when God captures our hearts, He has our mouths as well-- successfully bridling our tongues, and He can control our entire being.

So are you in a difficult situation now? Try singing, and imagine God saying to His angels, "That is my son (or daughter)! When they bless they are agreeing with Me. You never have to lift a finger to avenge yourself. We cannot bless and curse at the same time. We are either doing one or the other. A spout cannot give out sweet and bitter water at the same time. Nor can our mouth bless and curse in the same breath. It is schizophrenic and double-minded to curse one moment and then bless the next. James tells us that anyone who does this should not expect to receive anything from God.

"For let not that man think that he shall receive anything of the Lord. A double minded man is unstable in all his ways."
James 1:7,8

Recognizing that we may be cursing others is easier to do than realizing that we are cursing ourselves. Sometimes that is so subtle because we have become accustomed to it. Our bodies respond to what comes out of our mouths. God created our bodies to respond to what we speak. Seeing our bodies as a temple of the Holy Spirit is not always easy, especially when the mirror tells us that we do not measure up to the world's beauty and desirability standards.

"What? Know ye not that your body is the temple of the Holy Spirit which is in you, which ye have of God, and ye are not your own?" 1 Cor.6: 19

Feeling harassed, being afflicted with physical pain, and getting old can be opportunities for us to speak blessing over our bodies. Saying, "I bless the hair on my head; I bless this heart, knees, or back, because God's intention is not for me to be in pain", is like medicine over those ills. I have a relative (a woman) who has suffered from crippling arthritis for many years. She has a very bitter spirit and harbors much anger and hatred in her heart. She and her husband are born again Christians, but many years ago he had an affair and hurt her deeply. I cannot judge her heart, nor do I want to. There could be other reasons for the arthritis, but what she speaks is a great indicator of what is in her heart. My prayer is that God will bless her by removing the veil from her eyes, so that she can truly forgive and bless her husband. As a result, God can heal the two of them and their marriage.

Just as blessings come on us through our mouths, diseases and sicknesses may gain entry to our bodies the same way. So can detouring from God's natural design of blessing. I know of a case where ulcers have stemmed from bitter hearts habitually cursing everything that crossed their path. Our tongues are meant to release the freedom and blessings from God on the earth. Forgiveness, accompanied with blessing the one you have just forgiven, seems to be more effective in releasing freedom to both parties. We can say we forgive someone, but when we bless them with a sincere heart as if Jesus was doing the blessing, the soul ties that bound us to the unforgiving spirit are broken. Many people have found freedom in their marriages and other relationships when they learned to bless in place of old methods of cursing and temper fits. We have the kind of marriage we bless, or we have the kind of marriage we curse. We have the kind of husband or wife according to what we have spoken to or concerning them. The same with our children.

We can also reverse the curse by starting to speak edifying, encouraging, and uplifting words over our family, friends, and others; just as Jesus does over us. We can come to the place where the Holy Spirit is gaining control over our tongues, or rudders. This allows Him control of our ship---our whole being. We can begin to recognize the subtle forms of cursing in our lives, like giving up on something; we are cursing it. Jonah finding a ship going the way he wanted, appeared to be the blessing of the Lord, yet all the while, his destination was in the opposite direction, in Nineveh. What looks favorable to us may not be God's will or blessing. Blessing must be tied to the will and Divine nature of God. In Jonah's case, he was able to sleep in the boat because at the moment, it seemed as if he was getting away with it. However, his escape in the opposite direction could not be God's favor on him, because it was in opposition to God's purpose for Jonah and Nineveh.

I dare say that the reason some of us have not seen God's fullness in our lives is because we have not learned to bless what God has blessed. For the same reason people become despondent and bemoan the fact that nothing good is happening to them. There obviously has not been any investment into blessing others. We are promised that whatsoever we sow, we will reap. Blessing is seed that we are given to sow that will affect both the recipient and the giver. Since we know that God loves a cheerful giver, we can end this chapter knowing that He loves when we give blessing cheerfully.

PRAYER

Lord, I call upon You today. Please, bridle my tongue! Don't let my tongue be just in neutral so that I am not cursing or saying any bad thing, but help me to be engaged to say good things. I want to be a mouth of blessing that you can train and direct in the way that I should go. Please do not let my destiny be withheld because of an uncontrolled tongue. I repent and ask you to forgive me for the times when I had an opportunity to bless, but instead I chose to curse. Lord, I want to bless everything You died for. Let me be a person that shouts "grace" instead of shouting the problem. Let me also be a person that has the gift of God in my mouth.

    I pray that husbands and wives might bless each other physically, emotionally, and spiritually, Lord. I pray that I would bless everything that I come into contact with in my life. Wherever my foot treads, I pray that I would bless it and it would become blessed and holy ground, because when I bless You, it becomes exclusively Yours. I ask, Holy Spirit, that You put a guard over my mouth until it becomes like a rudder of a ship that you can turn in whatever direction You want, no matter how large it is. Let it be a tongue that is used to bless and is an instrument of righteousness. I pray that my tongue becomes an oracle that You can speak through, so that faith comes as others hear me blessing them. Help me to say what You are saying. Amen

CHAPTER 9

HE IS PITCHING HIS TENT

The Holy Spirit is beginning to unveil the mysteries of the kingdom by articulating and giving expression to spiritual thoughts with spiritual words.

"Which things also we speak; not in the words which man's wisdom teacheth, but which the Holy Ghost teacheth; comparing spiritual things with spiritual." 1 Cor: 2:13

It will be kingdom truth not taught by human wisdom, but the Holy Spirit granting the proper interpretation of spiritual truth through spiritual language. If we choose a receptive posture in this process, we will begin to understand His ways and His thoughts. The Lord is promising to reveal His thoughts and ways, which are much higher than ours, if we will only follow His prescription for a "higher way" of holiness. Words, when anointed, become a spiritual vehicle that transports us from one realm to another. In other words, the natural word becomes spiritual through the anointing of the Holy Spirit when we choose to speak words of blessing, instead of cursing.

In John 6:63 Jesus stated the words He spoke to them were both Spirit and life: "It is the Spirit who gives life; the flesh profits nothing; the words I have spoken to you are Spirit and life". Through the anointing of the Holy Spirit, words attain a spiritual life of their own. The spirit gives life to words spoken in blessing, which transforms them from the natural into the spiritual realm. At that moment, we discover the hope of our calling and the immeasurable greatness of His unlimited power and the power He has given us to bless others through us. Jesus Himself was actually representative of the "anointed" Word. He is the Word of God incarnate and He is the Messiah...which translated means The Anointed One. His anointing is the fuel that propels the vehicle. Without the anointing, the vehicle cannot operate properly. The letter kills (cursing), but the Holy Spirit gives life (blessing). 2 Cor. 3:6

For the ministered word to become spiritual food, it must proceed from the Lord's presence and perspective in an atmosphere of the anointing. As His anointing (His thoughts, His motives, His ways) are quickened within us, we can speak words of blessing over others from His point of view. When we fully understand that, then we are growing into His full stature and we can say...

"I am crucified with Christ; nevertheless I live; yet not I, but Christ liveth in me, and the life which I now live in the flesh

HE IS PITCHING HIS TENT

I live by the faith of the Son of God, who loved me, and gave Himself for me." Galatians 2:20

All our words should be galvanized with charity. Even if words of correction are necessary, when galvanized with charity, they will always be fruitful; love never fails. God's way is the best way, though sometimes it makes little or no sense at all in our minds. Yet it spares us from needless grief.

They were choking up as they read the letter from their two teenagers. In that letter there was healing, repentance, and joy. But it was not always like that. Not too long before that, this couple was beside themselves because their children were out of control and their family was on the verge of falling apart. These two children were rebellious and in trouble, pushing their home into a sort of war game. It became them against us, and vice versa. What happened to the sweet babies they had raised? One day, when they no longer knew what to do, they made a mutual decision to start applying words of blessing over their children. They grasped this truth with hope of getting their children back. They decided to bless instead of curse.

They began to replace angry words and expressions of disappointment with words of love and blessing---a difficult transition. Determined to walk this through, the parents hung in there and spoke blessings over their children. Then they saw it. There attitudes changed; their schoolwork improved, and peace came to their house. They knew that the war was over. Blessing was here. Jesus was in the house! The children, too, became blessers. Scribbled on that piece of paper that day were their words of love for their father and mother, expressing their changed hearts. They acknowledged and were grateful for the love of their parents, their goodness, and their refusal to give up on them. The once rebellious children had come home again. This miracle took place in a matter of a week!

God has already spoken. When He speaks today, it is to confirm something that He had already said before. His Holy Spirit never contradicts His Word. He carries it out with precise cooperation, just like He did at creation. God spoke and His spirit moved. Nothing materialized until God said it, which set in motion His Spirit to create matter out of nothing. God the Father spoke it, and the Spirit did it.

"The earth was formless and void and darkness was over the surface of the deep, and the Spirit of God was moving over the surface of the waters. Then God said, 'Let there be light; and there was light." Gen.1: 2-3

The Spirit listened for the voice of the Father. God's voice moved His Spirit into action. A definite connection existed between the "saying will" and the movement of the Holy Spirit. The authority of the Holy Spirit is based on the Father and the Son, for they are one. This is the triune--- the unity of the Trinity. This is divine agreement.

(Rev. 22:17) says, "come" (speaks it), and let the one who hears (Holy Spirit) say, "come". Did you see that the Spirit and the Bride are both doing the speaking and not just meditating

HE IS PITCHING HIS TENT

with good thoughts? In the previous testimony, both parents are expressing the heart of the Father. God's "dynamic duo" of the Word and His Spirit execute the spoken blessings of the Lord. We get to join into the same union. When we bless what the Lord blesses, we are agreeing with the Spirit. When someone curses what God has blessed, they are in conflict with the Spirit and are grieving the Holy Spirit of truth. People who are given to cursing are more likely to be deceived than blessers. Those who are submitted to blessing are in unity with the truth.

"If you abide in Me, and My Word abides in you, ask whatever you wish, and it will be done for you." John:15:7

To abide in us means to literally "pitch" His tent. He is not just going to be our neighbor, but He is moving in and taking over. When we pitch our tent in His Word, He will pitch His tent in our hearts. The Holy Spirit takes the logos (the said Word of God) and turns them into the rhema (the revealed Word of God or the saying Word of God), and it becomes revelation. God's words are spirit fabric, or substance. (see John 6:63) They have a life of their own, and they are powerful enough to transform minds with the life of God. Camping out with God in His Word is a position of blessing. He couldn't have made it any easier to find His heart and will. His words take hold of our hearts, and by faith, we speak them out. When we use the Word of God to declare blessing over a person or situation, the Spirit is released to work according to the blessing of the Lord. If you know of someone bound by drugs, you can bless them by declaring God's intentions over them as opposed to those who simply remind them of how horrible they are. Blessing does not focus on what is happening at the moment, but it is intent on what God originally intended. Cursing causes one to get off on a detour in life. Blessing releases the highway God intended them to travel.

There is a move of the Spirit of God when blessing is the motive of the heart. Without the Holy Spirit illuminating the Word of God, the word becomes a dead letter. To believe God's Word and that He is who He says He is, pleases Him. That happened to the centurion in Matt. 8:1-13. Centurion: "My servant is home sick even unto death". Jesus: "I'll go and heal him". Centurion: "No, I'm not worthy for You to come into my house". The centurion had faith that Jesus' words had power and authority even to the point of Jesus just speaking the word of life. "Just say the Word and my servant will be healed". Jesus: "In all Israel I have never seen such faith". Jesus was highly impressed with this Roman soldier, who was not a Jew, and not schooled in the scriptures. The one thing this soldier understood was authority. He recognized Jesus had authority that was beyond just the normal teachers in Jerusalem. His authority had power that brought about changes in the lives He touched with His words. Opposing what God has called good, brings us in conflict with Him. The power that is in blessing has authority to change the balance of circumstances in the favor of the blesser. Just send the word of blessing that is the will of God for everything He created. God declared everything He created in Genesis was good.

HE IS PITCHING HIS TENT

A PLACE CALLED JOY

Immeasurable, unspeakable the strength is the joy of the Lord. A peaceful home and loving family relationships are blessings that cannot be rivaled, like material wealth. Yet, it is still one of the riches of the Lord. The family we met at the beginning of this chapter experienced it.

"Blessed be the God and Father of our Lord Jesus Christ, who has blessed us with every spiritual blessing in the heavenly places in Christ." Eph.1:3

Joy comes with the Holy spirit and is a spiritual blessing. Like deep waters, it only needs to be drawn out and allowed to spring up.

True joy cannot be hidden. If it is there, it will show up whether we are trying to or not. It radiates on our countenance, and it lingers on those we come in contact with. With material possessions, we can blend in with the crowd if we want, but we actually wear joy. Joy knows no bounds, for it crosses all circumstances, and the settings do not limit or restrict it. Nor does it discriminate on social or economic status, age, ethnicity, or gender. The carrier of the joy is who matters. Sometimes it shows up in the oddest places. Joy is a believer's mark and evidence of God's Kingdom. It is also our strength that signifies separation from the world. Watch the faces of those in the world and read the message--- agony and depression. Does anyone have life and hope? Here comes the "church", the called out ones", and the world is searching

HE IS PITCHING HIS TENT

our faces. Are we any different? Or do we, too, carry the strain of the agony and depression that the world carries?

The presence of joy in our lives simply means that we have accepted God's loving kindness as a fact of our life. Joy exhibited is blessing released. This is the open door for people to see God's good intentions and purposes for us. Otherwise, they have nothing to hope for.

Joy is different from happiness. Happiness is based solely on happenings. If we had good news for the day--- that causes us to be happy. It is possible for one to get bad news and still keep joy. Joy is eternal.

"Then He said unto them, go your way, eat the fat, and drink the sweet, and send portions unto them for whom nothing is prepared: for this day is Holy unto our Lord: neither be ye sorry; for the joy of the Lord is your strength."
Nehemiah 8:10

Happiness is fleeting at best. Joy is an attribute of the nature of God. This is why it is described as the joy of the Lord, not the joy for the Lord. The lifestyle of blessing keeps a fresh download of joy continually pouring into the soul. We have been made an offer that we must not pass up. One who learns to bless, and bless often, changes a life of resistance for one of favor.

If you are facing something as hard as stone and it appears hopeless whatever you do, then before you give up

HE IS PITCHING HIS TENT

try this. Daily speak to the situation with the Word of God, knowing your loving Father in Heaven wants an outcome that glorifies. Dripping daily on the stone until it gives way to the will of God. Everything you need to live a life of blessing is available to you: the Holy Spirit, the word of God (living and written), an incorruptible seed with creative DNA, and a God that backs up His promises. Once you taste the benefits of blessing, no one can convince you otherwise. Just ask the couple who now have a peaceful home.

CHAPTER 10

IT IS OUR CHOICE

Why does it take more compliments to counteract one negative thought? It does not seem to take much to mess up a wonderful day. Why do we so instinctively lean toward the negative? You may be going about your day, perhaps singing, whistling a happy tune and just feeling absolutely wonderful. You decide to go shopping, and then you run into one of your neighbors and they say or do something negative to you... suddenly your beautiful, wonderful day is ruined. Whatever they said or did bothers you for hours. Consequently, you end up in a frenzy because one person was negative toward you. But wait! You have totally forgotten that ten other people complimented you that same day!

We empower whatever we set our minds and hearts to meditate on. To ponder God's word is to give it power in our lives.

IT IS OUR CHOICE

"Finally, brethren, whatsoever things are true, whatsoever things are honest, whatsoever things are just, whatsoever things are pure, whatsoever things are lovely, whatsoever things are of a good report; if there be any virtue, and if there be any praise, think on these things." Phil.4:8

Instead, we lay awake at night, tossing around in our minds what people said or did, and we empower the curse of those negative words that were spoken to us. Each time we chew on the negative too long, we move closer to the side of the cursor. That makes us more vulnerable to be in agreement with a spirit that opposes the nature of God. Inadvertently, such an agreement (whether we are aware of it or not) would bring an inheritance of the not so pleasant kind. Accepting an accusation and receiving it into our spirit, is letting go of what God has said.

By grabbing the lie, we lose our hold on the truth. We easily shrug off words like these; "God's hand is on your life and He has good things in store for you. He wants to do great things in the kingdom through you". To us, they become something nice that someone is supposed to say, even though they are true.

It is difficult to keep our grip on what is true if we are embracing a curse. Even in situations where we hear of other people's difficulties and pain, our reactions are a good indicator of whether we understand the heart of God when it comes to other people. Do we reject the desire to gloat over their hard time (especially if they had hurt us), or do we happily say or think, "I knew it! I knew it! They messed with me and God got them". This is hardly the heart of God.... and it is not the heart of a very good Father.

Choosing life or death is an ongoing process. We have to sift through all of the actions, situations, thoughts, and words that come at us daily. We can either take it or leave it. But they aren't always obvious, arriving with a label or announced, because we know that even if our friend offers us poison, and says, "I am your friend, drink this poison. You don't love me if you don't drink this poison". We would have no problem saying, "No", yet the deadly poison that would ensnare us with a destructive agreement may be subtle in its presentation, but packaged in the power of suggestion.

Avenues that spread the fear of diseases are numerous today, and we continually have to resist their onset. Never under estimate the power of words, even from seemingly innocent remarks. Thoughts that promote fear of the unknown are toxic and should not be given any time or space on our mental "to-do-list".

"As he (a man) thinks in his heart, so is he." Prov.23: 7

God is all about creating life and recreating Himself inside our minds so we can have the mind of Christ. Choosing life provides us with the ability to continually repeat the things that duplicate or multiply the life of His Spirit. If something does not speak life into our spirit, then we do not have to receive it, even if it is from our best friend!

IT IS OUR CHOICE

ARE WE REALLY HEARING?

How we hear God is an important aspect to receiving blessing. The Holy Spirit is constantly speaking to us about blessing. Mark 4:3-9 Take for instance the parables that Jesus spoke. To the outsiders, the stories of Jesus were just that- stories. The meaning and truth were hidden from them. Understanding the truth was their ticket to freedom, but although they were all ears, they weren't getting it.

> *"And when He was alone, they that were about Him with the twelve asked of Him the parable. And He said unto them, unto you it is given to know the mystery of the kingdom of God; but unto them that are without, all these things are done in parables; that seeing they may see, and not perceive; and hearing they may hear, and not understand, lest at anytime they should be converted and their sins should be forgiven them." Mark 4:10-12*

He really does want us to know the mysteries of the kingdom of God. The word mystery simply means it cannot be discovered by a casual glance. In other words, it means, "that which cannot be seen through natural understanding". Having an encounter in the presence of the Lord causes one to see the mysteries from the perspective of Christ, and then they are no longer mysteries. These mysteries help us or strengthen us to bless when the circumstances may cause us to want to curse the situation. Unbelief and suspicion do that, too. Have you ever received something from someone and your first thought is, "I wonder what they want from me"? People who have trouble trusting due to broken promises and perhaps being defrauded in some form will have difficulty receiving blessing bestowed upon them. God does not disappoint. Disappointments come from a preconceived idea that was never God's anyway. God is all about appointments, not disappointments. Blessing is filled with His intentions for your life that are backed up by His written word, but it is released as a catalyst when it is spoken or prayed over someone. Rejecting the blessing is not the only challenge. Temporarily receiving the blessing and then discounting its power and letting it go is another.

Believers can also take the Holy things of God (like a prophetic word) and cast them before people who are oblivious to the value. It is not a pretty sight when the swine trample the things of God underfoot. They lose out on the blessing, because someone who despised prophecy was more familiar with cursing than the power in blessing. They should not be surprised if they find themselves stuck in the same condition years later. Yet we were given a catalyst from God to get them unstuck and bring them into a fuller life of joy and abundance. Backing away from that word of blessing results in the maddening cycles just being repeated again and again. We need to contend for the blessing. Although it seems easier to believe the lie than the truth, both require a similar action- belief in something bigger than us. If the lie or curse is given life by believing in it, then it becomes bigger than we are, and before long it has taken the position of power to the point of consuming our hopes.

IT IS OUR CHOICE

So where will the seed of the word land in our life? On the roadside where it is exposed to the birds of skepticism? Where the sun can scorch and burn out any joy of life? Choked out by the cares of life? It does not have to be that way. It can land in our hearts in the fertile ground of faith. We can become skillful in handling truth through blessing, and this will keep us from being deceived by curses.

CHAPTER 11

THE HEART OF GOD'S KINGDOM

This is not an isolated story. It could be, and does happen anywhere sad to say. In an instant, everything had changed. He had been frustrated and enraged. The other car was not driving fast enough in the left lane to suit him. Nonetheless, they were not letting him pass, nor were they trying to switch to the slower lane. Agitated by this time, the man rammed the family vehicle. The car flipped into the face of oncoming traffic. Moments later he learned that every single person in the car was killed. His uncontrolled anger had now turned tragic and destructive. His road rage had turned what was to be a time of festivities into a nightmare.

The way of the cursers never find favor no matter how much they justify their reasons for their actions. For that man, his assumption that someone was obstructing his way, resulted in violent deaths. His anger stemmed from a life of cursing, and the road rage was simply another step in its progression. It cost him his inheritance and any blessing that was available to him. Had he been a blesser, the outcome could have been very different. Cursing in some cases is a matter of life and death physically; in other cases it is a matter of life and death of the soul.

Think for a moment about the parable of the prodigal son and his older brother. Even though the older brother faithfully served at home, he was resentful of his wayward brother. He was also resentful of the unearned love that his father had for this prodigal son. He had great difficulty when his brother came to his senses and was restored to favorable status and treated to a homecoming party. (see Luke 15: 11-31) On the same day, he was dumbfounded to learn from his father that he could have had a party the whole time. He could have been celebrating with his friends continually. He was not able to enjoy his inheritance due to the anger and injustice he felt toward his brother. His cursing kept him from a relationship with his father, and instead he settled for only a working relationship with his father.

He never discovered the intimacy he could have enjoyed with his father. His heart was poles apart from his father's. His nature was more familiar with cursing and judging only the circumstances, where his father's heart was inclined toward blessing. Since the father had a blessing heart, he was able to see by faith into the future and his son's return. The elder son had never understood his father's desire to bless his brother.

Our inheritance may be on hold because we don't see with

THE HEART OF GOD'S KINGDOM

eyes of blessing like our Heavenly Father does. The principle of sewing and reaping definitely fits here. When we curse by speaking against the mercy and will of God the Father, we are blinded from seeing our portion of the inheritance. Those who bless see things in the opposite spirit from that of the world system, which is more inclined to curse anyone who is not as miserable as they are. God's kingdom is relevant for today. Though we are in this world, we are not part of its system. The kingdom of God is a kingdom pronouncing good news. This world system, however, is pronouncing captivity through the culture of cursing. This way of life is filled with anger and a lot of mistrust. People who are aligned with cursing are more apt to deceive without remorse, because cursing hardens the heart to the point of callusing the conscience.

In the gospel of John this conflict of culture is confronted. (Matt.: 11-12) "From the days of John the Baptist until now, the kingdom of heaven suffers violence, and violent men take it by force". We usually think of violence as something that is militant and angry. The word violent (in the Greek, biadzo is translated) The idea is that when something fills up the space, it crowds out any dirt that happens to occupy the glass. When Jesus comes into our life, He will crowd out those things that are in opposition to His nature. The prescription for breaking a life of cursing is to be filled with the Holy Spirit who will speak from the nature of Christ.

The fruit of the Spirit is love, joy, peace, patience, kindness, goodness, faithfulness, gentleness, and self-control (see Gal. 5:22-23). These are attributes of blessing. It is interesting that they are referred to as the fruit of the Spirit. These qualities are developed in those who are willing to bless. Blessing doesn't leave any room for the dark side of cursing, because the art of blessing has a way of crowding out what does not belong. Cursing gets crowded out and finds no room to launch from.

Love and mercy, by contrast, are characteristic of His kingdom. They crowd out anger and false judgments. The culture of blessing and the culture of cursing are always at war. Blessing leads to faith and the pleasure of the Lord, whereas the culture of cursing leads to unbelief and condemnation. Ephesians tells us to put on the new self, which is created in the likeness of God; laying aside falsehood (cursing) and speaking truth (blessing) to one another. Don't give place to the devil. (See Eph.4: 25-28) The devil looks for opportunities to corrupt and pollute what God has blessed through cursing.

Many times when this happens to us, we fire back our missiles and before we know it, we have fought cursing with more cursing. We leave there feeling condemned. The only way to win this war is not to return evil for evil, but instead give a blessing. Nothing disarms cursing more than giving a blessing in return.

"Bless those who curse you; pray for those who mistreat you." Luke 6:28

There we have it---the strategy for overcoming the devil. The devil tries to bait us to fight evil with evil. Jesus says the victory is in the blessing. Remember, blessing is pronouncing God's intended favor upon them; not what they deserve. Blessed are the merciful; they shall obtain mercy. Blessing and mercy are partners, and when we sow them, we reap the favor they bring. I don't know anyone that does not need more favor or mercy.

Those who learn to bless skillfully will get to their desired destiny much quicker. Those who think their strength lies in their toughness of heart and mind to beat someone down with words are farther from God's plan than they know. Blessing is one way to show that we truly trust God, because we leave the outcome to Him. Cursing may feel good at the moment to the low end of our flesh, but the end result is that we have fallen into the same pit as our enemy. The devil's playbook contains the plan to get you to look at areas of unfulfilled desires and accuse God of being unfaithful to you. Does that sound absurd? Well, consider this--- complaining is one form of saying, "God, You have not done a very good job of taking care of me because of blah, blah, blah".

Complaining was the main thing that angered God the most with the children of Israel while in the wilderness. Rejecting blessing is to reject God's prophetic input in our lives. Have you ever noticed that sometimes when you try to bless someone they do the unworthy thing? "Oh, I'm so unworthy"! That's because some are so beaten down that any blessing placed on them will seem foreign. But we are to keep blessing, allowing the Holy Spirit to work and break through the shield of death around them. Once they are free, they will become a strong blesser.

God introduced blessing on to the earth through a man. He blesses one so they can in turn bless others. Blessing is generationally contagious. When a family starts a practice of blessing, it causes a reaction that will affect their entire home. It flows from the head of the house down to everyone else and out to the teachers, to the children, and on to their friends. Blessing cannot be stopped.

RECEIVE

Just receive the word of blessing and leave the rest to the Holy Spirit. Prophetic words that give life are to be believed, embraced, and watered by prayer. Mary, the mother of Jesus, did this (see Luke 1:38). Instead of trying to figure it out, she simply agreed with God. Believing and receiving the word of the Lord leaves no room for the enemy to play mind games as he did with Adam and Eve in the garden. He does so by asking us the question, "Did God really say..." When we believe God, our hearts are tender toward Him and we are good ground, ready for the seed of life. Instead of rehearsing threats or consequences, why not bless others with the potential of God's favor.

The old adage is true; "You can catch more flies with honey than vinegar". Some have used vinegar for years because they grew up on vinegar. Jesus wants us to get a taste of honey so we won't go back to vinegar. Why not try something like this? "God intends that you become successful and be a man or woman of God. You are going to rise up and call Him blessed. All the days of your life will be filled with great joy. Many will be blessed because of you". Imagine what a world of difference this would make.

"This commandment which I command you today is not in heaven, that you should say, ' who will go up to heaven for us to get it for us and make us hear it, that we may observe it'? Nor is it beyond the sea, that you should say, 'who will cross the sea for us to get it for us and make us hear it, that we may observe it'? But, the word is very near you, in your mouth and in your heart, that you may observe it."
Deuteronomy 30:11-14

When we are born again, we are born into a life of understanding the very nature of God. We short-circuit this when we make it too complicated. The will of God for us is to love Him with all of our heart, mind and strength, and out of that comes the structure that we hang the rest of the building on.

"You shall love the Lord your God with all your heart, and with all your soul, and with all your mind." Matt: 22:37

From this understanding, we become receptive. The fact of the matter is that we need to know how to receive the blessing. His words and promises are not up for debate, nor is He going to take them back. God so loved us that He paid the price for our redemption, so we might become all that is a reflection of Him. If we are delayed on our way to the promise, our fallen nature bends toward believing the fearful and negative.

THE HEART OF GOD'S KINGDOM

PRAYER

Father, bring to mind these things that hold our hearts and minds in chains. Today, we choose life over deadly words, and we choose to believe what You say about us. Since faith comes by hearing, not having heard, we need a hearing word today. Father, we have been eating of the tree of the knowledge of good and evil that is cursed; please forgive us. Today, we choose to start eating of the tree of life that has an abundance of blessing in its fruit. Thank you that You did not give us what we deserved, but You gave us what You desire. Forgive us for rejoicing when ill things happen to others.

CHAPTER 12

THE UNITED CHURCH

"Whenever they moved they moved in any of their four directions without turning as they moved. As for their rims they were lofty and awesome, and the rims of all four of them were full of eyes round about. Whenever the living beings rose from the earth, the wheels rose also.'"
Ezekiel 1:17-19

They never broke rank, nor did their heads turn as they moved. Faces pointing outward, they moved with the Spirit of God in that cycling of a wheel within a wheel (see Ezekiel 1:15-16).

None of the beings were tripping over one another, nor was one trying to promote itself over the other. They moved as one. If this isn't a perfect picture of unity, I don't know what is. Living and moving in unity as believers invites the Lord to show up. What does this have to do with blessing you may ask? Unity is an avenue for the release of blessing within a local body. God moves through and within His body. We are a "cluster" with the potential of being made into new wine (see Isa. 65:8). Yet break off a grape from the cluster and it becomes a raisin dried up with no juice. Therefore, to avoid damaged fruit and to create unity, these ingredients are necessary; proper connection to the vine; consideration for the ones you are connected to; communication with those who lead you, and cooperation for the purpose of the whole harvest.

Get together, assemble, and meet. That makes connection possible (see Heb. 10:25). Learning to get along happens while we fellowship and worship together. Opportunities are fostered there for proper connection to the vine. Part of the participation in corporate fun is learning about one another and allowing others into our lives. Also, we can shift from a mentality of someone owing us to sowing us. We never know when being present in the moment for someone is the difference between life and death.

With connection comes consideration---thinking more about how our actions affect those we connect with. Consideration knows how to function properly in a corporate setting. It is being aware of those around you, so they will not feel invisible. How we act in public is different than when we are alone. You can tell if you are considerate or not by how people feel after you have been there. Do you raise the level of peace and joy, or are they exhausted by your company? By understanding proper connection and being considerate of

THE UNITED CHURCH

how you fit within the group, you will have a sensitivity for how to bless.

Agreement within the local body does not mean that we get everyone on the same page. It is also not about everyone doing the same thing. But, it is about coming into the place where we are in agreement with what the Holy Spirit is saying. Walking in agreement simply means we are all looking for the same outcome. People get bogged down with the agreement of methods and lose sight of the final product. Different beliefs and interpretations of the bible have created enough tensions and dissensions among the cluster which takes away from the ultimate harvest. Being in unity with the Holy Spirit provides for an environment of blessings to overtake you. Ezekiel's description of the wheel shows how each creature is different with a different perspective, but when they move, those in the back of the wheel must trust the direction (though they are not in the lead) when there is a need for the other creatures to move in concert. The obedience of the group is more important than the individual identity.

Cooperation is working together as a body with the spirit of the Lord. He leads; we follow. We can be pleasantly surprised at how our personal desires become fulfilled in the process. In a marriage, unity is when a husband and wife are open to the leading of the Holy Spirit and allow Him to move them as one. My husband and I do not have to share the same views, but we are still in unity because we are still in union. We both want the same outcome--- to please the Lord. Cooperation is simply to act together for the same cause. Without cooperation, there will be no operation of the group. Blessing is a way of bringing together various parts of the body of Christ to accomplish the harvesting of the fruit. Success or failure for any venture lies in the unity of those who see the end result as more rewarding than any personal goal or agenda.

WHAT IS YOUR SCENT?

"How good and pleasant (how fragrant an odor) it is for brethren to dwell (and connect) together in unity. It is like the precious oil upon the head, coming down upon the beard, even Aaron's beard..." Psalms 133:1-2

Unity among brothers is sweet, and yes, this is the way things should be! In its absence, the odor of strife is repulsive to God. David, the man after the heart of God, yearned for it. His heart yearned for the presence of unity. He knew that unity created a blend that is agreeable and inviting, wonderful enough to invite God to come among them. Its scent is likened to the smell of the precious anointing oil--- God's signature fragrance. The Lord loves aromas! Moses was instructed to create the scented oil for the purpose of setting apart people and utensils that would be used exclusively for service. (see Exod. 30:22-25) The resulting combination of myrrh, cinnamon, cane, cassia, and oil made up a fragrance saturated in this oil. The high priest entered into the Holy of Holies to offer the blood of atonement for covering the people for another year. This anointing oil reminded David of the unity of brethren working together for one purpose. David

THE UNITED CHURCH

also said that where unity was, there was also commanded blessing of the Lord.

"Behold, how good and how pleasant it is for brethren to dwell together in unity. It is like the precious ointment upon the head that ran down upon the beard, even Aaron's beard; that went down to the skirts of his garments; as the dew of Hermon, and as the dew that descended upon the mountains of Zion; for there the Lord commanded the blessing; even life forevermore." Psalm 133:1-3

Notice that unity is an environment that invokes the blessing of God. That is why "a kingdom divided cannot stand".

"And if a kingdom be divided against itself, that kingdom cannot stand." Mark 3:24

Those who catch sight of what it means to bless and not curse will most likely experience the unity of the Holy Spirit and an environment that brings favor.

I remember someone years ago, sharing this very enlightening story to me about the art of creating the right perfume for the right woman. An expert perfumer explained to him in order to find just the right perfume for his wife, she would have to be there so she could match the perfume to her body. She explained that everyone's body interacts differently with the fragrance. She told him, "I can match it to your body chemistry, but not hers". Isn't that interesting? This is the unity of blessing; you have to be present for it to work through you. The commanded blessing can be created in a home by being present with the family so the chemistry of all the different parts can be blended for an aroma that anoints you for special use.

"And walk in love, (blessing) just as Christ also loved you and gave Himself up for us; an offering and a sacrifice to God as a fragrant aroma." Eph. 5:2

The fragrance is matched to the body of Christ--- believers who will release the aroma (the walk and talk in blessing others). Unity is a sweet aroma, but more than that, it is a powerful combination when mixed with blessing.

David pictured the anointing as the precious oil running down Aaron's beard and settling at the edge of his robe. The place it settled was on the fringes--- the most saturated point of the robe. The most potent and powerful aroma of the anointing was not on the head where it is poured, but on the skirt of the garment where it gathers. Before we speak a word, where does it start? Yes, in our thoughts. Therefore, if we spend time with God, praying and meditating on His thoughts and His ways, eventually we become Christ-like in thought, word and deed. Then His thoughts become our thoughts, and they run down to our mouth and finally saturate our self. We speak His words of blessing everywhere He appoints us. Just as the river flowing from the throne of God deepened, the farther away it flowed from its point of origin, so does the anointing (see Ezek.47:1-5 NLT).

Reaching the saturation point is crucial for the anointing because that is where signs, wonders, and miracles happen. And what are these signs, wonders, and miracles? They are the blessed life manifested in our relationships, health, finances etc. Walking the blessed life is the greatest testimony that will win the lost soul to Jesus and free us from the cares of this world and of self.

A certain woman who suffered from the issue of blood found that point of saturation (see Mark 5: 25-34). She was sick and she was broke. Her story could be anyone's story. Incurable diseases have the potential to kill hope and clean out savings; but Jesus was in town. Pushing her way into the croud, she reached out for a miracle and touched the hem of His garment. She found commanded blessing and life flowed into her body, breaking the curse of years of infirmity. When the Holy Spirit descended in the upper room and fell upon the disciples; they then became recipients of that saturation and blessing of the Lord.

Think of this in terms of releasing blessing. Whenever we bless something or someone, there is a saturation point to be reached for that blessing to take. The challenge is not to give up before we reach it. We do not know, nor do we determine, that point. For us, it is only to obey and keep blessing others in thought, word, and deed. Consistency is the key. Seemingly stubborn situations or difficult people most likely need more saturation in the blessing. Just as we continuously water whatever we want to grow. That targeted blessing saturates the will of God for that person until it is accomplished. God's rhema word (the revealed word of God) comes to us as we soak that situation or person with blessing, and He moves the situation from the impossible to the possible. The saturation point is not just for miracles, but the place for the flow of blessing. To reach that point, the anointing cannot be hindered.

"It is like the dew of Hermon coming down upon the mountains of Zion; for THERE the Lord commanded the blessing (barak- Hebrew- to speak the intention of God) --- life forever." Psalm 133:3

So, when God said "THERE", He meant where there is saturation; whether that is of unity or the anointing oil. It is a saturation of blessing. There is blessing and there is a commanded blessing. The first is blessing in a general way. Commanded blessing is specific. It is the Hebrew word, ISAVAH, which means "to release or send specifically a message to someone or something", or "to appoint or connect to, or enjoin". So, when I say, "I love you" to my husband, the impact of those words are greater for him than if I say the same thing to others. Such is the power of an appointed blessing.

"Commanded" also denotes "authority". The commanded blessing carries authority with it so that it will accomplish what it was sent out to do. (see Luke1:37). There is an anointing connected with the commanded blessing. It is a powerful anointing to bring life and freedom. And when

Isaiah declared that, "the Spirit of the Lord is upon me", he was not saying he was feeling chill bumps. It was more like "to smear with the anointing oil", as was in the case of Arron when the anointing oil ran down from his head. God's Spirit upon him brought an anointing with specific purposes--- to deliver the afflicted, the brokenhearted, the captive, and the prisoner. Today, believers live under the commanded blessing of the Lord. Our unity becomes the release of that commanded blessing and pleasant aroma before the Lord. When it comes upon us we begin to smell like Him. It is the scent of blessing with the sweetness of myrrh, meaning that we, the believers, have died to ourselves.

We could almost hear the Lord saying, "Aha! The death of my humanity is in this oil. Its sweetness speaks of Me"! It is no wonder that the Lord desires unity among believers. But just as the Lord is attracted to the aroma of unity, the enemy is invited by the smell of all that is contrary to God. Fear is an oder to the enemy. Anger and unbelief also attract him. If we allow these emotions and feelings to overtake us, the unclean spirits that attach themselves to these encourage us to continually feel that way, if left unchecked. The commanded blessing is not where cursing, division, and strife exist.

CHAPTER 13

THE COMMANDED BLESSING

What is there in God's treasures for believers to reach maturity and unity? Plenty! God's provision was encompassing, and provided full coverage for every stage of that new life. Paul had a revelation of this, and he wrote about it in the commanded blessing.

Apostles, prophets, evangelists, pastors, and teachers are commonly termed the five-fold ministry, serve the body for this particular purpose; to prepare believers for the work of the ministry and to edify them. (see Eph.4:12) Bringing believers to the unity of the faith, maturity, and the knowledge of Jesus is their goal.

"Till we all come to the unity of the faith and of the knowledge of the Son of God, to a perfect man, to the measure of the stature of the fullness of Christ: that we should no longer be children, tossed to and fro and carried

about with every wind of doctrine, by the trickery of men, in the cunning craftiness of deceitful plotting."
Ephesians 4:13-14 NKJV

How much of the "measure of the nature" we want in all areas of our lives is determined by us; whether we want alot or a little. And the measure is in the "fullness of Christ". The word "fullness" is the Greek word (pletto), which means that "there is no more room to receive, for every nook and cranny is filled." That's full! By setting the measure of blessings that we release from our lives, we also set the measurement for others to bless in return. The amount of God's power operating within us is determined by the degree that we come into His fullness. This principle works in some level even for the heathens. When they learn to bless others, it keeps on coming back to them. God cares about how we communicate with one another.

If what He is after is unity, then anything causing tensions or division is not pleasing to Him. It is not common for someone to say, "I need to tell you this in love", which is really code for, "I am going to unload on you". Speaking the truth in love was not meant to be the preface for giving someone a piece of our mind. Using this verse as a covering to criticize or straighten someone out is a misuse of scripture. Yet speaking the truth in love has nothing to do with filling them in on information. The word "truth" there is the Greek word (alethia), which means the "manifested reality". Since Jesus is the Way, the Truth, and the Life, it is easy to say Jesus is the Truth. The misconception is for one to think that when they are telling someone the truth, the person listening will grow. The verse read is the one who is speaking the truth will grow.

Now ultimately, the one listening to the truth--- Jesus being revealed--- will grow as well. Blessing is all about speaking truth as Jesus, the Truth, would have declared it. The one doing the blessing, or speaking the truth, will grow into the image of Christ. When we are just locked in on the facts of an issue, we may be blinded to the truth. Since truth is what Jesus is saying, facts may be about what the enemy wants us to see, and we end up cursing based on facts. Remember, cursing is placing something or someone in a lower place than Jesus did. Facts tend to do just that; lowering people below the potential that God has set for them. This does not mean we are in denial of the gravity of the situation. It does, however, mean we should not focus solely on what has been, but we should set our attention upon what can be done through blessing.

Cursing is not cussing, but rehearsing the threats to someone and what will happen to them if they don't change, is cursing. Pronouncing failure is a way of cursing or placing them in a lower view than how God sees them. The devil always wants to refer to our past, but God is prophetic. He wants to talk to us about our future. Continual reminders of past failures are a type of cursing because they are the opposite spirit from what Jesus wants us to see. Forgiveness was given to us to blot out the past; blessing is prophetic in that it points us to a future destiny and calling.

We were designed to be people that grow in response to love. Providing the right environment for something to grow is critical. Growth is the potential to come into what something was originally designed to become. A combination of the right ingredients enables a plant to grow because of its DNA. Provide all the right conditions and the environment will happily release the potential of the seed. Seed bears in itself the blueprint for its future. Right conditions for a believer to grow include speaking the truth in love and the watering of the word.

"Since you have in obedience to the truth purified your souls for a sincere love for the brethren, fervently love one another from the heart, for you have been born again not of seed which is perishable but imperishable, that is, through the living and enduring Word of God." Peter 1: 22-23

I have included a quote given to me from a very dear friend and brother in Christ. "Jesus said when we become born again, we are a new creature. New in every way. Spiritually, we have a new 'DNA', if you will. Pure, innocent and untarnished." Biting into the apple (or what ever it was) changed both Adam and Eve physically and spiritually because of the now changed makeup (DNA, if you will). Spiritually, they were no longer innocent. They now knew both good and evil. They also changed physically because something in the fruit changed their physical nature that caused them to begin to die. The death DNA was now introduced both physically and spiritually."

THE COMMANDED BLESSING

I personally believe that the tree of life was that they only spoke God's truth, because Jesus is the tree of life. So, when they spoke, they only spoke His word of blessing. After they sinned, they spoke words of cursing to each other because they had eaten of the tree of evil. The first thing they did as an indicator of this, was to blame or to curse. First Adam blamed Eve, and then Eve blamed the serpent.

Being born again means that we have new seed or DNA. God set the principle of how the seed works in the Genesis account of creation. God said the life is in the seed. We have been given life inside the seed of Christ that abides in us. Blessing waters the seed so it comes to its potential of full life. Cursing destroys faith and discourages the soul in becoming God's building. (John 3:9 Amp.) "No one born (begotten) of God (deliberately, knowingly, and habitually) practices sin; for God's nature (DNA) abides in him. (His principle life, THE DIVINE SPERM, remains permanently within him; and he cannot practice sinning because he is born (begotten) of God". As we grow into the image of God, His divine nature (His Spirit, our Teacher, guides us into all truth) and will strengthen us to bless, and not curse. Because we have become pregnant with His divine sperm.

We should consider the word of God, as a means to grow in His divine nature. Just as in our natural family, the more we spend time with our parents, we slowly take on their nature. The more we think on what God has in store for us, the more it can become a reality when we speak His word. We can turn man's fallen nature around when we consider the

Lord's perspective and what He wants to do, and agree with His word. Think what can happen when we choose to bless and honor His word above our own opinion.

There is no end to the miracles we can receive. Since we are responsible to provide an environment for growth through blessing and cursing, any conditions hindering or stifling that growth, such as demonic powers that thrive on cursing, need to be removed. They can cause the condition or environment to stagnate or fail to produce growth. Whether that is within a church, family, or work atmosphere, dealing with unfavorable conditions to a person's growth is paramount. Caring for the health and growth of today's church means that we learn to bless and not curse. That is, we bless with the truth. For blessing with the truth encourages spiritual maturity. Ultimately, we grow to a place where we are like Jesus, who exhibited a deep, unwavering trust in His Father.

Sometimes I have been asked to pray for people, and I begin to declare a blessing of healing over them. They keep interrupting with more information, mostly what the doctor has said. They are so focused on the information that they cannot hear the pronouncing of the blessing of healing. The seeds of faith are so planted in such a way that they cannot help but water them every chance they get. I ask them to listen to the word and set their hearts on living and not dying. I have no problem with doctors telling a patient the facts, but when we believe God for a miracle, we must set aside the information and hear the blessing of transformation.

THE COMMANDED BLESSING

"For this reason I bow my knees to the Father of our Lord Jesus Christ, from which the whole family of heaven and earth is named, that He could grant you, according to the riches of His glory, to be strengthened with might through His Spirit in the inner man, that Christ may dwell in your hearts through faith..." Eph.3:14-17; NKJV

The word grant means, "here is my God-given potential, or what my intention is". Again, God has good intentions toward each one of us. Seeing that God-given potential come into fruition for someone is a cause for celebration. Paul also understood that strength in our inner person is vital. We are strengthened in the inner person through blessing. Blessing is God's power coming through the Holy Spirit in the inner person.

"That you, being rooted and grounded in love, may be able to comprehend with all the saints what is the width and length and depth and height--- to know the love of Christ which passes mere knowledge; that you may be filled with all the fullness of God." Ephesians 3:17-19 NKJV

The "fullness of God" encompasses all four dimensions; width, length, depth, and height. Length and breadth alone are not fullness. We need all four aspects. By becoming like Christ in every aspect of our lives, we begin to live life like He did---as overcomers of the world. Consequently, we no longer specialize in one aspect of our faith, such as only ministering faith or healing. We can function in every aspect of Christ. That is because, as the body of Christ, we respond to the will

THE COMMANDED BLESSING

of the head--- Christ.

We become blessers, just like Jesus. We begin to look at people and life through His eyes of grace and hear things the way He hears. That is the unity of the spirit in the bond of peace (see Eph.4:3). A consorted movement together of Christ's body can bring an unparalleled release of the glory of God. Such an environment invites God to show up and do the impossible. It enables us to repel demonic power, heal the sick, cast out demons, and invoke the blessing of God.

PRAYER

Lord, we are so thankful that You have given us a freshly spoken word to bless the body and the house of the Lord. God, we want to get this inside of us. If we don't get anything else, we want to get this down in our spirit. Let it not be just another message that comes and goes and tickles our ears, but let it become part of the fiber of who we are as those who bless what You bless. We want to be connected to Your cluster and be a blessing to those to whom we are connected. Amen

CHAPTER 14

WHO IS RULING

Conquests are exciting for the conquerors, but ruling may be another story. The greater challenge between the two is to rule, because that calls for the continual dominance of whatever was conquered. Ever heard of a man who can make a million dollars but cannot keep it? Money rules the man. Though he can conquer the idea of making money, he cannot rule money. What we can conquer, but cannot rule, produces frustration and disappointment. Cycles of constant ups and downs in a christian's life may be a reflection of this reality. This is true in our external and internal worlds.

"He who is slow to anger is better than the mighty, and he who rules his spirit, than he who captures a city."
Prov.16:32-33

Solomon wrote Proverbs, and he understood something

about ruling. Ruling ourselves is priority. Whatever we need to overcome, remember there is a reign to follow, which determines longevity. If we cannot rule ourselves, we are sure to lose any ground we gained. The length of our story in the place we conquered is determined by whether we can rule.

"Like a city that is broken in to and without walls, is a man who has no control over his spirit." Prov.25:28

The picture is of a city without protection. When we think of this in regard to our life, any inability to govern ourselves becomes an invitation for the enemy to harass and exact a toll on us; drawing us to the curser's side. This is a matter of having self-control and keeping our emotions in check, especially anger. We are responsible for how we respond to life's surprises. The enemy of our soul will be more than happy to control our emotions if we let him. He has sought to rule over our emotions since the garden of Eden. In that place of perfection and innocence, the serpent was able to find an inroad into the heart of man through sin. Jesus Christ through His death and resurrection restored the power to conquer and rule, beginning with ourselves. However, the struggle is still ongoing.

Even before humankind, satan wanted to rule everything; he was vying for the right to rule. Rebelling against God with a third of the angels was the result of his pride. His rebellion against God, however, cost him his place in heaven, and he was cast down to earth. It was one of several times that the devil would be thrown out of heaven.

WHO IS RULING

"By the abundance of your trade you were internally filled with violence, and you sinned; therefore, I have cast you as profane from the mountains of God. And I have destroyed, O covering cherub, from the midst of the the stars of fire. Your heart was lifted up because of your beauty; you corrupted your wisdom by reason of your splendor. I cast you to the ground; I put you before kings, that they may see you."
Ezekiel 28:16,17

"How have you fallen from heaven, o star of the morning, son of the dawn! You have been cut down to the earth; you who have weakened the nations!" Isaiah 14:12

The book of Revelation gives us a peek into the conflict in heaven. It was a heavenly place where satan could enter and make accusations to the Lord against believers. Scripture refers to Lucifer or satan as "the prince of the power of the air". (Eph.2:2) "And there was in heaven, Michael and his angels waging war with the dragon. The dragon and his angels waged war, and they were not strong enough, and there was no longer a place found for them in heaven. And the great dragon was thrown down, the serpent of old, who is called the devil and satan who deceives the whole world; he was thrown down to the earth, and his angels were thrown down with him." Rev. 12:9

Satan lost the war in heaven and was cast down to earth, which before the creation, was called the planet of darkness. That heavenly place that he had access to was no longer available to him.

WHO IS RULING

The word "place" in Revelation 12 means "land". It is the same "place " in Ephesians where Paul told believers not to "give place to the devil". (see Eph. 4:27 NKJV). In essence, the devil lost ground to stand on in heaven. God loves land. It is no wonder that He is so jealous over the land of Israel. He encourages His people to buy the land, keep the land, and hold the land. The parable of the "Pearl of Great Price", tells of the need to buy the land that the pearl was buried in. It is one thing to overcome, but then it is up to us not to give anymore ground--- not a handhold, toehold, or foothold to the devil. Glance back to the Israelites' entrance to the promised land. In order to rule that land, they had to drive out the Canaanites, the Perizzites, and any other pagan idol worshippers. (see Josh:3:10) Co-existing with them was not an option. Blessing and cursing cannot exist side by side. James writes that blessing and cursing should not come out of the same mouth anymore than sweet and bitter water can come from the same fountain. (see James 3:10-11)

"Now the salvation, and the power, and the kingdom of our God and the authority of His Christ have come, for the accuser of our brethren has been thrown down, he who accuses them before our God day and night."
Revelation 12:10

The devil may have lost his place in heaven, but he looks for places in earthen vessels from which he can curse God and His family. He does not cease to accuse us to the Father. "Accuser" is a way of saying "curser". Satan is the curser of God's children. If we pronounce failure and judgment on someone, it is in the category of being an accuser. It's no wonder that God is not pleased with us when we curse someone. Satan lost his place in heaven as an accuser. We can certainly miss out on the favor of God through cursing what God has blessed.

The devil's list of accusations and questionings are endless: "how could you love them he asks? Don't you see what they did? How could you deliver and save a people that turn their back on You? How could you treat someone so mercifully when they are so cold toward you"? Satan is legalistic---- he looks for cracks to accuse us as unfaithful or disobedient. He will work through others to pronounce judgments of condemnation on us. Psalms says, "blessed is the one that does not sit in the seat of the scoffer". (see Ps.1:1) Blessed are those who choose another seat than the seat of the scoffer. Scoffing means to belittle or make small something that has value (to make fun of). Cursing is similar in that it devalues what God has blessed. If you find yourself without blessing, maybe you should evaluate your seating arrangements.

HIS BLOOD SPEAKS

Since that devil roams around the earth looking for those who are easy prey, we have to deal with his schemes. But we are not without protection from him, nor do we lack power to defeat him.

"And they overcame him because the blood of the Lamb and

because of the Word of their testimony, and they did not love their life even when faced with death." Rev.12:11

The blood of Jesus is the protection and the word of our testimony is a weapon. The believers gave evidence in the above scripture that they were saying the same thing as God. Their testimony is the same as when Jesus was on the earth. Jesus, when confronting the devil in the mountain, used the Word; He testified by saying, "It is written". The blood of Jesus was the payment in full that has set a barrier between the family of God and the devil.

When we say what Jesus has said in His Word and claim our inheritance because of His blood, we have the power to defeat the devil. The devil cannot take any ground where we are blessing, that is, saying what Jesus would say. The battle is won through the blood of the Lamb and blessing what Jesus has blessed through His sacrifice. He is the ultimate victor and rightful ruler of all that He conquered. Jesus overcame sin, the world, death, and the accuser. The blood that Jesus shed, cries out to the Father to defend and cover us with His protection. Just as Abel's blood cried out to God in his defense against Cain, his brother.

"And Cain talked with Abel, his brother; and it came to pass when they were in the field, that Cain rose up against Abel, his brother, and slew him. And the Lord said unto Cain, where is Abel thy brother? And He said, I know not: am I my brother's keeper? And he said, what hast thou done? The voice of thy brother's blood crieth unto Me from the ground.

WHO IS RULING

And now art thou cursed from the earth, which hath opened her mouth to receive thy brother's blood from thy hand".
Gen.4:8-11

In God's eyes, when we curse or accuse our brother or sister, it is the same as murder to Him, and the blood of Jesus cries out to Him in their defense. Then He comes rushing in to protect us and to defend us. Not because of ourselves; but because of the blood of Jesus. Imagine the powers of darkness on the morning of Jesus' resurrection when they saw Jesus rising out of the grave! They understood the authority and the blood of Jesus. The bible names Jesus as the first born among many brothers. Jesus is our big brother in the family of God. (see Rom.8:29) That blood continues to speak today. Every demon knows that the blood covering is over every believer in Christ, and it validates their claim to overcome and rule as believers. When a believer declares the power of the blood, its authority is released.

Jesus possessed the authority to not just whip the devil, but the authority to rule over him for eternity. Satan attempted to get Jesus to use His authority to satisfy His own hunger. He was trying to tempt Jesus' flesh after fasting forty days. Jesus was hungry. Satan offered all the kingdom's of the earth for one moment of worship, or the temptation to turn the stones into bread. Jesus answered quoting from the book of Deuteronomy, "it is written, man shall not live on bread alone, but on every word that proceeds out of the mouth of God". (Matt. 4:4) Though Jesus had the authority and power to turn the stones into bread, He chose not to use His authority for the flesh.

Overcoming has nothing to do with how cleverly we phrase our words or how loud we can holler at the devil. God's inspired and inerrant word that has passed thousands of years of testing is our weapon of choice. Hanging between heaven and earth on that cross, Jesus was faced with the choice of cursing or blessing. I think satan thought he had Jesus defeated. With the crowd wanting the execution of an innocent man, along with the taunts of "He saved others, but He can't save Himself", Jesus chose to bless them even from the cross. With His last breath, He asked for forgiveness on their behalf. We really know the power of blessing is a reality when we can bless while being confronted with shouts of cursing. Jesus overcame with His blood and the word of blessing. It was as if satan was taunting Him and saying, "Come on, curse me. Do You see what they have done? You came to Your own people and they did not receive You; You are nailed".

Jesus saw the eternal plan, and "for the joy set before Him, endured the Cross". (Hebrews 12:2) He looked past the moment of cursing and pain and saw the glory that He had in the beginning with the Father. If we could at times look past the circumstantial evidence against us and see what happens when we bless, I think we would be able to endure a little longer before taking the bait to curse. Pleasing His Father was better than getting out of the momentary pain. Though heaven awaited His command to come to His rescue (that option was certainly available to Him), Jesus refused to use His authority for self-gratification. We are today victorious because He blessed and did not curse that day on the cross. Our authority through the blood of Jesus that cries out and speaks on our behalf to God our Heavenly Father, is uncontested.

Be A Winner!!

    A brother in the Lord, who I will call Ken, shared about a book that promoted the idea of cursing whomever or whatever you don't like. Church people were cursing anyone they disliked, including cars and trees! Fear was the driving force behind this motivation. Are you a determinator (a play on Ken's words) or a terminator when it comes to blessing? He said a determinator is determined to bless, no matter what anyone does in return. They are not moved by the immediate circumstances. A terminator cuts off a relationship when there is any hint of resistance. The determinator will win out through blessing. A terminator has a lot of burned bridges and numerous short term relationships. If it is worth fighting for, it is worth blessing to win. At the very least, blessing is close to the heart of the Lord, and you will feel the pleasure of the Lord when you bless and keep from cursing. With the small snapshot of Stephen, we are given in the book of Acts, we get the picture that he had the heart of a determinator. Isn't Ken's play on words interesting? I just had to include his thoughts in this teaching. He has applied God's principle of speaking and walking in blessing others for many years, and is truly a blessed man for doing so. I appreciate his permission to include his thoughts in these lessons.

WHO IS RULING

Stephen was full of faith and of the Holy Spirit (see Acts 6:5). Stephen's ministry was powerful enough to get the attention of the religious people due to the signs and miracles that were happening through his ministry. He confounded the religious leaders with the spirit of wisdom and the spirit in which he was speaking. They were so threatened by losing control of their domain that they set a conspiracy against Stephen. Dreaming up false accusations, they had Stephen dragged before the religious council to stand trial. In his defense, Stephen recounted the history of the Jews and ended with a scalding rebuke of the religious hearers.

"You men who are stiff-necked and uncircumcised (outside of covenant) in heart and ears are always resisting (set on what you believe and will not hear) the Holy Spirit; you are doing just as your fathers' did (living under a generational curse). Which one of the prophets did your fathers' not persecute? They killed those who had previously announced the coming of the Righteous One, whose betrayers and murderers you have now become; you who received the law as ordained by angels, and yet did not keep it." (Acts 7: 51-53)

After that public address, Stephen's audience was fit to be tied. They hated the truth, and the man who dared to say it so much, that they rushed at him gnashing their teeth--- not a pleasant sight. In their mind, there was one way to silence such a man, and that was death. But Stephen gazed up to heaven and saw the Glory of God. Jesus was standing at the right hand of the Father.

WHO IS RULING

"Behold, I see the heavens opened up and the Son of Man standing at the right hand of God; But they cried out with a loud voice, and covered their ears and rushed at him with one impulse. When they had driven him out of the city, they began stoning him; and the witnesses laid aside their robes at the feet of a young man named Saul." Acts 7:56-58

This is a mature believer filled with faith and determination. On the verge of death, he did not react to the crowd's hatred. Instead of cursing them for their rejection, Stephen saw Jesus and blessed them by pronouncing the will of God, which was to forgive them. In my mind, I picture Stephen catching sight of Jesus, and then doing what he saw Jesus doing. Wow! That will get the endorphins flowing.

"Then falling on his knees, he cried out with a loud voice, 'Lord, do not hold this sin against them'! Having said this, he fell asleep." Acts 7:60

What a powerful thing! Stephen fought against the natural human tendency to withhold blessing and forgiveness from the mob. He didn't call out and say, "Lord Jesus, get me out of this mess! I did not bargain for this", or "I've been serving food; don't I deserve some perk out of this"? Stephen saw the one who broke the power of the curse, so his focus was not set on the accusers, but the blesser. Instead, his glimpse of the Lord in His glory gave him strength to bless the conspirators and executioners. Stephen became a witness to the truth--- that greater is He who blesses than he who curses.

WHO IS RULING

We never know who we affect when we choose a blessing stance. Paul, the Apostle, a man who God greatly used to write a third of the New Testament, was at the stoning of Stephen as a young man. That event had to have made an impression on Paul's (Saul at the time) mind (see Acts 22:20). Later on, when Paul was faced with angry, resistant people, he also chose to bless and not curse.

On another occasion, Paul and Silas were beaten and thrown into prison for giving a young slave girl freedom from a spirit of divination. Paul and Silas began singing praise to the Lord instead of complaining about their circumstances. Other prisoners listened to them pray and sing hymns. Then suddenly, at about midnight, the jail experienced an earthquake that caused the prison doors to open. Revival broke out and the jailer and his entire household were saved. While other prisoners were cursing their captors, Paul and Silas became the thermostat for the rest of the jail and changed the temperature from cold-hearted to a red-hot revival. You can change your situation if you will bless at all times and let His praise be continually in your mouth.

When we are waiting on The Holy Spirit there is much that we experience. The time frame varies. Blessing is a final step in forgiveness. I can forgive every day, but when I bless, I can begin to see them through the eyes of their Creator and Father. Somehow, things begin to look differently. When you bless people, you can feel their heart. It is as if the Lord pulls back the reality covers and we can see things from another vantage point. Yet the more I have blessed, the more I have felt mercy for those who have hurt me. That is truly the power of blessing. We are not alone in our struggle in this world; nor are we without hope. Winning through blessing was the way Jesus overcame.(John 16:33 NKJV) "In this world you will have tribulation; but be of good cheer, I (Jesus) have overcome the world". When we find that we are constantly blaming other people for issues, whether it is on the job or at home, there is a good chance we have not grasped the revelation of blessing. Blessing means that in the midst of chaos, we can still see Jesus and we choose to bless. Hearing about someone else's pain and suffering or what they are saying about us is only bait the enemy uses for cursing. Carrying the spirit of cursing is like being a magnet--- you attract more of the same. Cursing pushes the pause button and we are frozen in time, held back from moving into our destiny or divine favor.

"Nothing ever connected", my sister in the Lord said through her tears. Life had been a bitter pill. I could see the hollow look in her eyes many times before. The look of one who has lost all hope of the miracle ever happening. She had experienced her share of disappointments, and at this juncture in life, she had moved from hopeful to survivor mode. One night she remembered what I had told her about blessing your enemies. She repented for her attitude of cursing. She asked God to forgive her, and she forgave her husband. Her whole countenance changed.

It was evident that this was her freedom moment. The realization that things could change for her fueled hope for the first time in many years. Her change was so dramatic to those of us who knew her that it started to catch on when another and another followed suit. She had been cursing her family, especially, her husband. She had blamed him for all the problems they were facing. She had questioned if God could ever do anything good in his life. Not until that night could she expect any change. She too, quickly repented to her husband for her actions and for being in agreement with a cursing spirit.

Pride keeps us from our own blessings; that is why God hates it. Pride points fingers at others, our past, how we were brought up, etc. God knows it is locking us out from being blessed. His intentions are only for our good.

PRAYER

Father, I thank you for the power of the Holy Spirit that allows us to enter into the blessing of The Lord. At this very moment, we want to be free from those whose words have hurt and wounded us. We know that nothing can bring division and strife unless we give it life. We ask that the power of Your grace would deliver us and cause us to be an instrument of blessing in word and in deed. Amen

CHAPTER 15

RESURRECTION POWER

Up to now, we have discussed the benefits of blessing--- it honors the Lord as well as releases our inheritance in the Lord. I must confess, like most people, I used to use the term blessing to describe a feeling or a state of being. If someone was doing well and things were going their way, they would say, "I am blessed". I have since come to realize blessing is a lifestyle and a position of being covered by the favor of the Lord. However, we have to distinguish the feeling of blessing from the obedience of blessing. We can do this by comparing the words "happy" and "joy".

Happiness is based solely upon happenings. It is an emotion or feeling we get when what is happening in our life is agreeable with us. When something good, like a promotion comes, we are happy. Joy, on the other hand, is an attribute of the Holy Spirit. It is part of His character. It is not based on the need for something happy to rejoice about.

RESURRECTION POWER

"The joy of the Lord is our strength." (Neh. 8:10).

Notice that it does not say, "the joy for the Lord". The joy comes as a direct impartation from the Lord through the Holy Spirit. This kind of joy is a result of trusting the Lord in every happening of life. The joy of the Lord is a constant. Even while things are not necessarily happy. Happiness may be momentary or fleeting at best, but the joy of the Lord is a sense that God is constant. We are full of His joy, even though we don't understand what is going on at the moment.

Blessing is similar because it is not based on things, like whether we feel like we are blessed, or in fact don't feel like blessing anyone. Blessing should be a constant in our life much like joy. Blessing is also an attribute of Christ; after all. He died to free those who are under a curse. Blessing is not about a feeling--- whether someone we don't particularly like deserves to be blessed or not. I am thankful that Jesus did not wait to get the right feeling before He was willing to die for me and for you.

I don't think that Jesus was necessarily happy about going to the cross. We can see this by the prayer He prayed in the garden--- for the cup He had to drink to pass from Him if possible. Jesus also prayed, ... "Not My will (happiness), but Yours be done". (Luke 22:42) We also read in (Hebrews 12:2) that "Jesus, the author and finisher of our faith, endured the cross for the joy set before Him". We can see that the joy He saw kept Him moving toward His destiny. I believe the joy Jesus saw was the glory that was going to be restored to Him at the right hand of the Father after the cross.

Sometimes blessings may have to die to our own will. However, the joy that follows is the power of God released to do His will; to bless and not curse. Resurrection is connected to blessing. The resurrection is the victory whereby we did not fall prey to cursing or passing judgment on who deserves it, is a gift that we can give. That is why we can forgive ourselves. Like blessing, we can give it as a gift or we can withhold blessing and choose life through the resurrection. Likewise... we, through the power of blessing, can choose life over death, blessing over cursing. The power of blessing is truly the redemptive kind.

The Third Cup of Blessing

There were four cups of wine at one feast. This was the Jewish Passover. During this feast, four cups of wine were drunk to commemorate the Israelites' journey as a people and God's promise to them. The first cup of wine was taken to remember what the Lord had done. Coming out of Egypt to the Promised Land was an event never to be forgotten. No other people saw the protection and provision of God as strongly as the Israelites. Pouring a small amount of wine into the cup, the Jews drank it and stated something to this effect: "Lord, we remember that You brought us out of Egypt". The second cup of wine was drunk as a remembrance that they would never be slaves again. Years of backbreaking labor in Egypt were to be a memory and only that. Then the third cup, the one most of people are familiar with because of communion, was the one, which Jesus chose to make His prophetic declaration. This was the cup of redemption; also known as the cup of blessing. The fourth cup of wine symbolized the prophetic promise given to Abraham that they would be a people and a nation.

The Israelites' story of deliverance from Egypt was ratified in that third cup. It was viewed as the blood of the Lamb! Smeared over the doors of the Israelites' homes, the blood kept them safe from the spirit of death that moved through Egypt. Taking the firstborn who were not covered by the blood. (See Exod. 12:13) The Egyptians came under judgment by being cursers that defrauded and enslaved the Israelites. God had promised Abraham that He would bless them who blessed him and curse those who cursed him. (See Gen: 12:3) This certainly held true to Abraham's seed as well. The Egyptians were experiencing the God of Abraham returning their curses back on them. The telling and retelling of the deliverance story was now the Israelites' mandate for generations to come. Their enemies heard of their miraculous freedom. It struck fear in their hearts. Who wanted to go to war with a nation whose God cared for them like that?

This is what stands out to me: How prophetic it was for Jesus to choose the third cup at the Passover meal! With the cup of redemption, He announced a new covenant between God and humanity. Jesus could have chosen any of the four cups for remembrance, but He chose the cup of redemption. Paul refers to this as the cup of blessing. (See 1Cor.10: 16) The cup Jesus drank from--- or in a truer sense, the cup He would demonstrate was the crucifixion. I think it is interesting that this "Cup of The Cross ", if you will, was called The cup of blessing. Jesus went to the cup of blessing to set us free from the power of cursing.

The principle of blessing is still relevant today. Within it, we can break the power of a curse through the power of blessing. Blessing always triumphs over cursing. Which side of the cross are you on? The side of blessing that destroys the curse. or the side of the curse that is in opposition to the work of the Lamb? The connection is that when we take the cup of blessing, we come under the new covenant. Gone is the veil that separated us from God; we can now have access to all of God's promises. What they had in the Old Testament was a mere shadow of it. Take a little time out to read.
(Exodus 12:3-7)

The Israelites had to choose a lamb without defect for the Passover feast. It was imperative that the lamb was without blemish, for it was a type of Christ. Each lamb was inspected before the family could prepare it for the feast. Once a lamb was selected, the family brought it into the home where they would become familiar with the sacrifice. At the right time, they killed the lamb by slitting its throat and placing its blood on the doorpost. The house was now identified with the blood; its inhabitants were safe from the destroyer. What a perfect picture of Jesus! It was what He was about to go through after He took the cup of redemption, blessed it, and drank it. None of His disciples could fully understand the eternal value of what they were seeing right before their eyes. Chosen as

RESURRECTION POWER

God's pure Lamb, Jesus was about to give up His life to save many from destruction. This blood is still active today.

Coming together as believers in a communion service symbolizes what has taken place in both the spiritual and natural realms. The Lamb of God was slain, and because of His blood, we are free from the curse. We are given a new nature and we are bound by something stronger than death itself through the blood of Jesus. Under the new covenant, we can now be a blesser and not a curser; just like Jesus was and still is today. I think picking up your cross and following Jesus entails picking up the cup of blessing and following in His footsteps. Nothing annoys the devil more than someone who will not take the bait and curse. We all are called into this celebration of Passover; daily celebrating the life of Christ through blessing those He has blessed.

(1 Corinthians 10:15-16) I speak as to wise men; you judge what I say. Is not the cup of blessing which we bless, a sharing in the blood of Christ? Is not the bread, which we break, a sharing in the body of Christ? A definite yes! The act itself is symbolic of an actuality. By drinking the cup, we are partaking of our covenant through the blood of Jesus. God produces an inward transformation in us where we become people of blessing. He wants to infuse every part of our life, so when we speak as a voice for Jesus, it affirms the cross of blessing. Blessing then becomes not just something we use as a greeting, but an instrument of power. As freely as we have received blessing, we should as freely give it.

RESURRECTION POWER

There was one conversation with His disciples where Jesus alluded to the idea of blessing as a lifestyle. What they had wanted were positions and places of authority. What they got was a challenge.

"And He said to her, "what do you wish?" She said to Him, "Command that in Your Kingdom these two sons of mine may sit one on Your right and one on Your left". But Jesus answered, "You do not know what you are asking. Are you able to drink the cup that I am about to drink"? They said to Him, "We are able". He said to them, " My cup you shall drink; but to sit on My right and on My left, this is not Mine to give, but it is for those for whom it has been prepared by My Father." Matthew 20: 21-23

Jesus was referring to His crucifixion when He asked them if they were able to drink the cup He was about to drink. The word "cup" was referring to cursing.

The Lord's table was intended to be more than just a Christian ritual. By taking the cup during communion, we are participating in the cup of redemption, which is the Lord's heart to bless. Though the act of communion may be restricted to a time and place, the extension of blessing is not. We could be at home, work, the bus stop, the jungle, in an airplane, in a submarine, you name it, and still bless. Blessing knows no bounds. Every time we bless, we are remembering what Jesus has done. As you extend the cup of blessing, you will see how you are marked for destruction to pass over you.

RESURRECTION POWER

A promise was made to us during that Passover. Jesus said that He would not drink again of "this" cup until He drank it with us in His Father's Kingdom. At the consummation of the marriage supper of the Lamb (Jesus), we are going to drink of this cup again. He is waiting for us to join Him in this celebration none has ever experienced; until then, we have an engagement. This pledge is best understood in the context of the Jewish culture. When a young Jewish man wanted to marry a girl, he would get permission from her father. If he was permitted to ask her, he took a cup of wine and went to her house. He would extend to her a cup of wine. If she took the wine he, too, would drink. This was to signify her acceptance of his marriage betrothal. We are waiting for His return and the finality of our covenant with Christ. We have drunk the wine and we are saying we will be faithful to Him until He comes.

God places great value on the marriage covenant, announcing that what he puts together, no one should separate. He has blessed and betrothed us to His son with the cup of blessing: a better covenant, overcoming power, blessing, and a pledge from the Bridegroom Himself--- one day, we will drink this cup with Him at the glorious marriage feast. No other celebration since the beginning of creation will compare.

CHAPTER 16

A HOUSE BLESSED

My prayer echoed from the corridors of time; "I plead the blood of Jesus over my family". These are words that ran down through the years over them. Those were words that I prayed frequently. Little did I realize how powerful that declaration was. You see, I was declaring the cup of blessing. My words mean more now than ever before. Blessing invokes the blood covenant over a house and family. When we enter a house, let our peace be upon it.

"And into whatsoever house ye enter, first say, peace be to this house." Luke: 10:5

If our peace comes back to us, it is like an echo indicating that there is no peace or fellowship/communion there. What if it is our own home that has no peace? Then we go through the house and bless it.

"And if the Son of peace be there, your peace shall rest upon it; if not, it shall turn to you again." Luke 10:6

You speak, "My peace be upon you! Peace is upon this house"! The Lord will come and invoke His covenant right over that home. It is as if He is saying, "I've written My name in this house and nothing deadly will enter". Cursing invalidates the covering, because cursing is in opposition to the work of the cross and of blessing. We cannot speak words such as, "There is evil in this house; it is full of evil spirits. Nothing ever goes right; it is full of hatred and anger". We cannot declare this and then expect God's peace to be there. We are cursing it instead of declaring God's blessing over it. Since with blessing comes peace, we can also conclude that with cursing comes the lack of peace and well-being. James tells us not to be double minded; a double minded person is unstable in many ways.

"Let not the one who is double minded think he will be able to receive anything from the Lord." James 1;7-8

A double-minded person thinks one way at one moment and another at other times.

What if we see someone sin? John clarified this. When we see someone sinning that does not lead to death, we are to ask for life. (That means the person is not hardening their heart against God, nor are they blaspheming or denying the will and purpose of God) We now know that blessing is speaking life, and cursing is speaking death. Asking God for life for the one sinning is not that we are agreeing with the sin, it's speaking the intended restoration as to where they should be. The bible tells us that it is not God's will that any should perish, but that all should come to the knowledge of Christ. (See 2 Peter 3:9) If anyone sees his brother committing a sin not leading to death, he (those who are seeing) shall ask and God will for him give life to those who commit sin leading to death. There is a sin leading to death; I do not say that he should make request for these. (John 5:16)

Condemnation of the sinner may be the natural response, but choosing to bless; (and I don't mean to just say, God bless you, but to speak words of life into that person's life). By doing this, we resist being the judge, jury, and executioner. However, we remain confident that when we pray, our Heavenly Father hears us because we have not used our prayer to curse them. Who's Your Source? God likes being our protector and provider. Unless He is the One who captures our hearts as our main source, supplier, and provision for every area of our life, there will be a vacuum that will be filled by something else or someone else. God is the ultimate blesser; there is no one else that compares.

Thus says the Lord, "cursed is the man who trusts in mankind and makes flesh his strength, and whose heart turns away from the Lord. For he will be a bush in the desert and will not see when prosperity comes, but will live in stony wastes in the wilderness; a land of salt without inhabitant."
Jeremiah 17: 5-6

Another side of the curse is being blinded to God's ways. I can truly tell you that part of the blessing of the Lord is being able to see opportunities when they are sent your way. One who is living under a curse feels as if nothing good ever comes their way, and everybody else has the opportunities. They are blinded due to the curse.

God sent the prophet to the widow whose family was facing bankruptcy and slavery to pay off their debts. (See 2 Kings 4:3-4) In her eyes, she had nothing of worth to keep her family alive. What she did have, she made available to the prophet for multiplying. She obeyed the word of the Lord, and poured what little she had into other vessels. (other people) The oil continued to increase as long as she had other vessels to pour into. One who is constantly cursing those who are more successful usually feels victimized by society. They tend to feel they have an entitlement to what others have. The only way to break this cycle of cursing is to start blessing and speaking over others what you would like to inherit for yourself. Blessing will break the generational cycle of cursing over your life.

"Blessed is the man who trusts in the Lord and whose trust is the Lord. For he will be like a tree planted by the water when the heat comes; but its leaves will be green, and it will not be anxious in a year of drought nor cease to yield fruit."
Jeremiah 17:7-8

Notice the contrast between these two verses and the two before them. One refers to the curse on those who only trust in mankind, and the other is blessed when he trusts in the Lord. It's the picture of a tree. Not just any tree, but a strong and secure tree with presence and roots deep near the water source. So let the heat and drought come! Let the wind blow! With roots firmly planted and absorbing life, they are not moved. Fear and anxiety are not driving them to the wrong sources. Security for them comes from God's presence and their association to the River of Life.

Satisfied in the Lord and their relationship to Him, they are alerted to pending times ahead. Can you see how worry isn't even a factor? Yes, they are happy! Why not? There could be a drought going on, but their leaves are green and they are bearing fruit! Others benefit from your blessed life. Remember, that was the promise to Abraham--- that he would not only be blessed, but that he would be a blessing to all the families of the earth. Maybe you are to be the first one in your family to break out of the cycle and start blessing and becoming a tree planted by the River of Life. Begin the day with blessing and end it the same way. We all need the power of blessing. Remember the old adage that says to keep doing the same things and expecting different results is insanity? Well, cursing is insane.

PRAYER

Father, I release conviction in our hearts and a commitment that we are going to be a house of blessing and a people of blessing. We resolve to speak those things that we have need of and sow them in righteousness and faith to our children and the next generation. As proverbs 31 says, "our children will rise up and call us blessed"!

Father, we present ourselves to You as living sacrifices. We want to be holy and acceptable. Let the words of our mouth and the meditations of our hearts be acceptable in Your sight. Forgive us, oh God, for our coarse joking and brutal or idle conversations that tear down without building up. Cause us to extend Your cup of blessing to those around us from this point forward. Amen

A PRAYER OF BLESSING OVER YOUR HOUSE

This is the house of the Lord. It is Bethel; it is a place of blessing. The peace of God rules and reigns here. No unclean spirit shall be able to have any place here as I cast out every spirit of strife, division, and discord. I cast out the spirit of poverty. I invoke the blessing of the Lord upon my husband, my wife; and upon my children. My children shall be taught of the Lord and great peace shall be upon them. No weapon formed against them shall prosper.

"Every voice raised in judgment shall be found to be false. For this is the heritage of the children of the Lord."
Isaiah 54:17

CHAPTER 17

A HEDGE OF BLESSING

Then the Lord said to satan, "have you considered My servant Job, that there is none like him on the earth; a blameless and upright man who fears God and shuns evil"? So Satan answered the Lord and said, "Does Job fear God for nothing? Have you not made a hedge around him, around his household, and around all that he has on every side? You have blessed the work of his hands, and his possessions have increased in the land". (Job 1:8-10)

This is a spiritual reality. There is a hedge of blessing and of protection that comes through Jesus for you and your house. It is invisible, but it is there. As we pray, the Lord will put a hedge around us, our family, our household, and around all that we touch and all that we have.

A HOUSE BLESSED

"The angel of the Lord encampeth round about them that fear Him and delivereth them." Psalm 34:7

You can visualize this as a bubble of glory. There is an atmosphere around you that has a force. It carries a presence and power, and promise of heaven. Negative things (curses) can be all around you, but as they encounter that bubble, they hit a barrier they can't penetrate (the blessing of God's hedge of protection). Within that sphere, the blessings of God will come as well as increase. It carries a vibration of heaven that brings everything else into harmony with God's plan and purpose.

It has been known to happen that the land of praying farmers who declared God's Word has been protected and well watered; when all around them there was drought. It's the same with individuals--- trouble all around, but it won't touch you. Now, you may ask, how do you walk in this? First, it comes through Jesus. He became a curse that you might walk in the blessings of Abraham. What is that blessing? His presence living in you and through you. Where His presence is, everything else has to bow. The more we make His presence (speaking what He says) a priority, the more we become congruent, or in agreement with Him; the more the atmosphere around us becomes saturated in His glory.

BUILDING THE GLORY BUBBLE

There are specific ways we can build a hedge of blessing. First, steward your atmosphere. Be faithful to instill the disciplines that are part of living a healthy, fruitful, and vibrant spiritual life. Spend time in the Word, prayer, praying In the Spirit, worship, and fasting on a regular basis. Stay plugged into a local church where you are fed and cared for by spiritual leaders. Keep a childlike faith and expectation. The more you practice these things, the more you will stay in joy, praise and thanksgiving. You will find yourself in the glory bubble. Speak the Word of God into that situation.

"I am alert and active watching over My Word to perform it." Jeremiah 1:11

God wants to do His Word. He wants to bless us. His Word is alive, active, and full of power. Do not underestimate the power of God's living Word. What you say makes a difference. Your words have power. Agree with faith, not fear when you speak. Stay in the glory bubble.

Confess the blessing of the Lord over your children. Speak in harmony with God's truth. Release life, shalom, and wholeness. Appoint angels. Welcome the angel of the Lord to encamp around you, your family, your children.

"For He shall give His angels charge over you, to keep you in all your ways." Psalm 91:11

"and when the servant of the man of God arose early and went out, there was an army surrounding the city with horses and chariots. And his servant said to him, "Alas, my master! What shall we do?" So he answered, "do not fear,

A HOUSE BLESSED

for those who are with us are more than those who are with them." 2 Kings 6:15-16

My friend Connie (not her real name) related this true story to me years ago. Her children are all grown now, but at this particular time when her son Eddie (also not his real name) was a young teen and still at home, they were living in Texas and they lived in the country. In order to have fun with his friends they had to take a bus into town. At this time, their city had a curfew because there had been a crime wave caused by street gangs. Eddie was always very good about keeping the curfew and getting to the bus stop on time.

One particular night, Connie had gone to bed and had fallen asleep. She was awakened very early in the morning and she knows it was the Spirit of God, who had awakened her. She sensed an urgency to pray a hedge of protection over her son. She knew about the power of speaking blessings over her family. Once she had prayed she felt God's peace and went back to sleep. The next day, she was going from room to room doing her housework. She noticed that Eddie was following her around. She finally asked him if anything was wrong. Connie said he just looked at her and said he and his friend had experienced something unbelievable the night before.

She thought right away of how God had awakened her to pray a hedge of blessing of protection around him. He then told her that they had left the place where they had been a little later than what they should have. They had walked as far as they could to the bus stop. It was late at night and very dark. On their way there, they heard many footsteps behind them. The faster they walked, the faster the footsteps were. In spite of how fast they walked, they missed the bus.

They looked back, and a gang was following them. When they looked back again to the bus stop, there suddenly "appeared" right in front of them a police car. Then, a tall, large man stepped out and looked at them. He didn't say anything to them. He just motioned for them to get in the car. Eddie saw and felt the love of God in his eyes. The gang had witnessed all of this, and they turned and ran in fear. There was no fear in Eddie though, only the peace of God. They didn't even have to tell him where they lived. He never said a word to them and took them straight to his house.

They stepped out of the car, and when he and his friend turned to thank him, the man and the car vanished right before their eyes. Connie teared up as she shared this story and has been very grateful to God for His blessing of protection over her son and his friend. She knew that God had allowed them to enter into His glory bubble where the angels dwell. She knew and spoke His Word, and trusted that His Word would perform what it was sent out to do.

I mentioned before to define yourself in the Lord. What exactly does this mean? When David returned from battle in 1 Samuel 30, he and his men discovered that the enemy had burned their town, plundered their goods, and taken captive their wives and children. His men immediately turned on

David in anger and despair to stone him. What did David do? He strengthened himself in the Lord. Once he got back into His presence, it was like he stepped back into the bubble of God's glory. He was no longer defined by the empty village streets and the smoke that burned his eyes and nose.

He was defined by God's presence, and he got God's strategy for victory—"Pursue, overtake, recover all". You are going to possess the promises of God, but you are going to have to take them. The enemy will try to discourage you. You may face a reality that looks like complete defeat. You may even be attacked. But there is another vibration that you can take into where the living glory brings a different message and a higher reality. In the glory, opposition, becomes opportunity for great victory.

Take Your Place

"So I sought for a man among them who would make a well, and stand in the gap before Me on behalf of the land, that I should not destroy it; but I found no one." Ezekiel 22:30

As we welcome the anointing, we are to make up a hedge of blessing on behalf of the Lord. When your family and friends have a need, God has called us to stand in the gap. We are conduits for God to bless them through us. Every Christian has a hedge, but there are times when the enemy will pick on certain churches, families, or people, and this leaves a gap. We need to stand there and pray. When you see gaps, don't curse them, don't point them out and throw darts and condemnations. Come to their aid and run to the place of battle to defend that person with mercy and the blessing of God. If they are doing wrong, God does not mean for us to forgive and accept the wrong, but to speak a blessing over them. For example: "Lord open up the eyes of their heart. Holy Spirit convict them that they may repent of their wrong doing". Praying this way releases God's intentions over them and sets us free from judgment, or condemnation. This is the "standing in the gap type of blessing".

This is true on an individual as well as a corporate and national level. God has given each of us the authority and the calling to be the change agent or vehicle of His blessing for our families, our cities, and particularly our nation. The glory is permeated with the mercy of God, and mercy is permeated with His glory, compassion, and grace. (Exodus 33)

Like Moses of old, the presence and favor of the Lord in our life is not about our personal dreams and destiny. It is about stewarding that anointing for the destiny God has for an individual or our nation. If you see a weakness or wickedness in your nation, stand in the gap. God requires this of us. Pray a blessing over our nation instead of speaking words of cursing over it. God wants us, His children, to be vessels that He can speak through to bless and not curse. Build up a hedge of prayer and intercession. Fast and pray according to 2 Chronicles 7:14.

"If My people, which are called by My name, shall humble themselves and pray, and seek My face, and turn from their

wicked ways; then will I hear from heaven and will forgive their sin, and will heal their land." 2 Chronicles 7:14

We must not only speak God's Word, but be a doer of His Word in order that God may activate the blessing.

" But be ye doers of the word, and not hearers only, deceiving your own selves." James 1:22

"Watch and pray that ye enter not into temptation: the spirit indeed is willing, but the flesh is weak." Mathew 26:41

You see, in the weakness of our flesh, we want to "get even", so if we don't spend time in God's presence, then when something comes along to hurt us or offend us; we will curse instead of bless. Then we are placing ourselves outside of the glory bubble and out of God's protection. In other words, we must practice and apply the love of God, the blessed life, and not just preach it.

"My little children, let us not love in Word, neither in tongue; but in deed and in truth." 1 John 3:18

Ambassador of Glory

"now then, we are ambassadors for Christ." 2 Cor. 5:20

We are becoming ambassadors of the blessings of the Lord. We are a treasure in an earthen vessel. No matter how much darkness, the light will prevail. Jesus came to give life.

A HOUSE BLESSED

The thief comes to kill, steal, and destroy. He is a curser. Sometimes the very circumstances in which you find yourself are not about you, but about positioning you to carry the reality of God's protection and grace into that place of chaos and darkness. You may not feel like it, but you are an ambassador of life and glory. You are a carrier of the blessing. You are a carrier of Christ in you! The Lord is with you; His glory is with you. The situation may be dark and growing darker, but it doesn't matter because I Am that I Am is standing with you. I Am, Jehovah Raphe, your Healer. Jehovah Jirah, your Provider. Jehovah Rohi, your Shepherd. Jehovah Sabbath, the Lord of Hosts. The I Am is the source of the anointing of blessing, of provision, of healing. We are His representatives and we carry His blessings wherever we go.

When Jesus comes, every demon in hell bows! Often, we are the only link to the Lord in a bad situation. God is raising up an end time army with healing in our mouths, the spoken Word of blessing and deliverance in our mouths, and His Glory on our faces. It has very little to do with you. It is Jesus. So don't be a person who goes into a hopeless situation and pray, "if it be Thy Will". Jesus said:

"All authority has been given to Me in heaven and on earth. Go, therefore, and make disciples of all the nations, baptizing them in the name of the Father and of the Son and of the Holy Spirit, teaching them to observe all things that I have commanded you; and lo, I am with you always, even to the end of the age." Mathew 28:18-20

A HOUSE BLESSED

The government is on His shoulders. Have faith in the name and authority of Jesus and release the power of the blood of the Lamb. The power to speak blessing, and not cursing.

God has a purpose and a destiny for you here and now. There are demonic principalities that would like to hold people, regions, and nations in terror and fear. The only people who can make a change are the praying, believing saints. Let us arise, shine, and build a hedge of blessing, protection and glory around our families; our work places and communities; our churches, and our nation.

" Death and life are in the power of the tongue; and they that love it shall eat the fruit thereof." Prov. 18: 21

Let Us Pray

Father, I thank you for the power of Christ that operates in and through us. We stand in the family name and a Christ-given name by the Spirit of God. We choose to stand on the mountain of blessing. We stand to bless and speak over our nation and our families, declaring on earth that the United States of America is a nation under God. We bless the president, the cabinet, and those of various political affiliations. We thank You, God, for the power of grace that operates through Your Word of blessing. We refuse to live on the mountain of cursing. We defeat every curse with a blessing. We thank You Lord, that we have been grafted in, born of the Spirit of Christ and born into the family of blessing. Amen.

CHAPTER 18

THE BLESSING OF FORGIVENESS

Reasons We Need To Forgive

We all have a story to tell, don't we? An unfaithful husband or wife; maybe an abusive parent? Could it be that you can't forgive what was done to your son or daughter. What about the person who lied to us, or about us, or the person who believed those lies? These are all legitimate and justified reasons to be angry or hurt. But to God, nothing is legitimate enough to hold unforgiveness.

We experience real pain when we are hurt by someone; especially someone we love or have a close relationship with. It is often harder to forgive when the one who has been hurt is someone we love deeply, like our children. What is the first thing our flesh really wants to do? If our offender would put on sack cloth and ashes as a show of repentance, it would be

THE BLESSING OF FORGIVENESS

much easier to forgive them wouldn't it?

Remember, at the foot of the cross no one seemed very sorry. There was no justice at His so called trial. They shouted at Him, mocking Him. Shouting "crucify Him". They hurled insults at Him, mocking Him and saying... " So you who are going to destroy the temple and build it in three days, come down from the cross and save yourself"! (Mark 15:13,29,30). What was His response?

"Father, forgive them; for they know not what they do."
(Luke23:34)

If you stop and think about it, nine times out of ten, a person doesn't have full knowledge of the wrong they did. Because when a person has the fullness of truth they will keep from doing wrong. I believe that is one reason that Jesus forgave us all at the cross.

He knew that they (as well, as us) did not have full knowledge of things that we do or take part in until His light comes in to teach us right from wrong according to His truth. What does all this have to do with blessing, you may be asking? Well, when Jesus forgave them, He was actually speaking a blessing over them.

What does forgive mean? It means to give freedom from payment...before an offence is actually done! We are to learn to walk in a lifestyle of daily forgiveness even before anyone says or does any wrong toward us. Daily setting free

THE BLESSING OF FORGIVENESS

from payment what may be due. Jesus had already forgiven them way before His crucifixion had even been thought about or taken place.

The word forgive is actually two words. The word for, signifies something that took place ahead of time. Such as the word foretold. This tells of an event before it happened. Or forerunner; this is someone who lived before us. The other word is give. Forgive; to freely give before the action takes place. We are to walk in a state of forgiveness. Now you may be saying, well, that's all well and good, but how do we apply that to our daily life and why should we? Yes indeed, why? One word; obedience! God said so. Obedience equals power.

"But made Himself of no reputation, and took upon Him the form of a servant, and was made in the likeness of men. And being found in fashion as a man, He humbled Himself and became obedient unto death, even the death of the cross. Wherefore, God also hath highly exalted Him and given Him a name which is above every name: That at the name of Jesus every knee should bow of things in heaven, and things in earth, and things under the earth..." Phil.2:7-10

God highly exalted Him. He gave Him power over the enemy, death, hell, and the grave". In verse 9, God Highly exalted Him. When we forgive, we get blessed by receiving power over the enemy. When we forgive, we are empowered to be good representatives of the Lord. It keeps us from taking vengeance. Instead, we are given power to win the battle over

THE BLESSING OF FORGIVENESS

satan and we become the victors over what he tried to do. We set our offender free, as well as ourselves. We bless them, and we are blessed. When we obey and choose to forgive, it is an offering unto God. We release the power of God through us to teach others what His kind of love is all about. We release His anointing.

Unforgiveness affects our faith. It will not work if we don't forgive. (Mark 11:25-26) We block the flow of blessings in our life. To forgive is divine. It is a holy act.

How soon should we forgive? Quickly! Paul said:

"At my first answer no man stood with me; I pray God that it may not be laid to their charge." 2 Tim.4:16

He could have held a grudge, resentment, and a bad attitude. We know when we truly have forgiven if that person or persons names are mentioned and we have an attitude of responding with Godly love. We show that we are not harboring things in our hearts.

"O generation of vipers, how can ye, being evil, speak good things? For out of the abundance of the heart the mouth speaketh.' Matt.12:34

"Not withstanding, the Lord stood with me and strengthened me; (power from God) that by me the preaching might be fully known and that all the Gentiles might hear, and I was delivered out of the mouth of the lion." 2 Tim.4:17

THE BLESSING OF FORGIVENESS

He was given power over the enemy and we receive that same power from God when we forgive from our hearts. We, too, set our offenders free .

In the Lord's prayer, we get to the part where Jesus prayed... "forgive us our trespasses as we forgive those who trespass against us, and lead us not into temptation, but deliver us from evil". I always wondered why He prayed "lead us not into temptation, but deliver us from evil". Well, one day I asked the Lord what that meant. Shortly after I had asked Him, I was watching Perry Stone, (a very well known preacher and evangelist). Guess what he was teaching that day? He was teaching about the Lord's prayer, and specifically, the part I was wondering about. He went on to explain that the reason Jesus prayed, "lead us not into temptation", is because if we don't forgive, then we will be taking on the spirit to sin also, and we will not be delivered from the evil one. He will have victory over us and neither I nor my offender will be set free. Isn't that amazing? If you ever want to strike at the devil where it will totally disarm him, then choose to forgive the one who has wronged you. It is a mighty weapon against the lion. Remember, forgive quickly just as Jesus did and just as Paul did.

You see, I believe that what pleases God the most and impresses the world is a changed life for which there is no natural explanation. It is not what we say, but who we are. It's walking it out God's way. God looks at unforgiveness as spiritual dirt in the inner being. Now what are the consequences of unforgiveness? Well, instead of blessings, we have curses.

THE BLESSING OF FORGIVENESS

God only wants good for us. So it is for our own good that we must forgive. It can effect our health.

"The strong spirit of a man sustains him in bodily pain or trouble, but a broken spirit, who can raise him up?"
Prov.18:14

"For as often as ye eat this bread and drink this cup, ye do show the Lord's death till He comes. Wherefore, whosoever shall eat this bread and drink this cup unworthily, shall be guilty of the body and blood of the Lord. But let a man examine himself, and so let him eat of that bread and drink of that cup. For he that eateth and drinketh unworthily, eateth and drinketh damnation to himself, not discerning the Lord's body. For this cause, many are weak and sickly among you and many sleep." 1 Cor.11:26-30

Unforgiveness is sin. It can cause depression; it causes torture in our lives. And something that God hates, and that is that it can and does cause division.

If you don't forgive, you are delivered to the tormentors. What kind of tormentors? I mentioned some, like depression, and division. Also, lack of joy, unhappiness, heaviness of heart (weights on your spirit). You are poisoned. It hinders your worship.

"Therefore, if thou bring thy gift to the altar, and there remember that thy brother hath ought against thee; Leave there thy gift before the altar and go thy way; first to be

THE BLESSING OF FORGIVENESS

reconciled to thy brother, and then come and offer thy gift."
Matt. 5:23-24

We cannot love with unforgiveness.

"And above all things have fervent charity (love) among yourselves; for charity shall cover a multitude of sins."
1 Pet. 4:8

"Forbearing one another and forgiving one another; if any man have a quarrel against any; even as Christ forgave you, so also do ye.' Col. 3:13

If you don't forgive, you open a big door to the devil.

"To whom ye forgive anything, I forgive also; for if I forgave anything to whom I forgave it for your sakes forgave I it, in the person of Christ; (vs.11) "Lest satan should get an advantage of us; for we are not ignorant of his devices.'
2 Cor. 2:10-11

"Be ye angry, and sin not; let not the sun go down upon your wrath: Neither give place to the devil." Eph. 4: 26,27

When you don't forgive, you give the devil a foothold. What is a foothold? It is a base of operation that allows the enemy to advance to a stronghold!

God will not forgive us. Matt. 6:15 We block the blessings—the promises (gifts from God will not flow) because we are holding on to unforgiveness. We block our personal relationship with God and the ability to enjoy His presence, and our prayers are hindered. We are delivered to the tormentors.

If we don't forgive, we are doing the same thing that the man in Matt.18:33-35 did. He had asked his master to forgive him of a debt that he owed, and he was forgiven. But he also was master above others and when his servant came to ask forgiveness of a debt owed him, he refused to forgive. How do we turn the curses into blessings? The answer is still the same. Forgive, and do it quickly.

What is true forgiveness? It is being aware of what someone has done and still forgiving them! We achieve this level of forgiveness when we acknowledge what was done without any denial or covering up—and still refuse to make the offender pay for their crime. This doesn't mean we are to cover up and excuse, and not lovingly confront a wrong. We are not to refuse to acknowledge what happened. That would be denial.

Total forgiveness is painful. It hurts when we kiss revenge goodbye! It hurts when we think that the person or people are getting away with what they did and nobody else will ever find out. But when we know fully what they did, and accept in our hearts that they will be blessed without any consequences for their wrong...we begin to be a little more like Jesus changing into the image of Christ. How? God gave us a will to choose what we do with our actions. The act of choosing has nothing to do with feeling. It is strictly obedience unto the Lord. It is a God given ability to make choices. It is not a feeling. At least not at first, but is instead an act of our will.

STRENGTHENED BY GOD'S WORD

(1) We can choose to keep no record of wrongs. (1 Cor.13:5)

(2) Choose to refuse to punish. (1 John 4:18)

(3) Choose not to tell what they did. When I recall that total forgiveness is forgiving others as I have been forgiven, I remember;
    a. I won't be punished for my sins.
    b. Nobody will ever know about my sins. For all sins that are under the blood of Jesus will not be exposed or held against me.

(4) We can choose to be merciful. (Matt.5:7)

(5) We can choose to be gracious. True forgiveness shows grace and mercy at the same time. Graciousness is shown by what we don't say, even if what we say could be true. This shows maturity. The word gracious is translated "gentleness". It comes down to our English word graciousness.

(6) We can choose not to be bitter.

THE BLESSING OF FORGIVENESS

What is bitterness? It is one of the most frequent causes of people missing the grace (gentleness) of God!

"See to it that no one misses the grace of God and that no bitter root grows up to cause trouble and defile many."
Heb.12,15

What are the consequences? Bitterness manifests itself in many ways, but, the absence of bitterness allows the Holy Spirit to be Himself in us. This means that we will become like Jesus. Giving bitterness up is an open invitation for the Holy Spirit to give us His peace, His Joy, and the knowledge of His will. This is extremely important when it comes to the matter of reconciliation.

(CURSE) Unforgiveness, creates bitterness, and that gives the devil a foothold that becomes a stronghold.

(BLESSING) Forgiveness gives the Holy Spirit the freedom to bring restoration. It must first take place in the heart or it is worthless.

"out of the overflow of the heart, the mouth speaks".
(Matt.12:34)

If we have forgiven in our hearts, but that person or persons will not speak to us, we can still have the blessing of victory. It may be easier to forgive when we know that those who hurt us or betrayed us are sorry for what they did, but if we must have this knowledge before we can forgive,

THE BLESSING OF FORGIVENESS

we may never have the victory over our bitterness. It is a chosen privilege to be godly. To be like God and to pass this forgiveness on to someone else.

What is the very best reason to bless others with total forgiveness? Because we prize intimacy and fellowship with the Father more than we desire to see our enemies being punished. We want God's anointing too much to pursue getting even.

(Lev.19:18) "Thou shalt not avenge nor bear any grudge against the children of thy people (our brothers and sisters in Christ, or anyone), but thou shalt love thy neighbor as thyself: I AM THE LORD".

Comfort your heart with the fact that the Savior has Himself experienced all the trials He asks you to endure. (Heb.4:15 and 1 Cor.10:13)

I want to leave you at the end of this lesson with a quote from a gentleman named Brian Adam,.who is a well known author and writer. *"Faith moves God, but forgiveness releases His power."* We are not only to forgive people, but we are supposed to walk in forgiveness every day, putting it on like a cloak over the top of our armor.

Time To Pray:

Our Father, who art in heaven. Hallowed be Thy name. Thy kingdom come, Thy will be done on earth as it is in

THE BLESSING OF FORGIVENESS

heaven. Give us this day our daily bread, and forgive us our trespasses as we forgive those who trespass against us. And lead us not into temptation, but deliver us from evil, for Thine is the power and the glory forever and ever. Amen

CHAPTER 19

BLESS YOURSELF

Blessing is a means to confront issues in our life that are weaknesses. Four times in Revelation 2:7, it says, "to him who overcomes, I will grant to eat of the Tree of Life which is in the Paradise of God."

To overcome is the opposite of "to endure". It is God's way of introducing and increasing authority and maturity in our life. In the times of the kings in Middle Eastern culture, kings would go to war over territory and superiority. Gaining wealth and spoil was done through conquest against a real king. When a king conquered a city or another king, he would ride through the streets placing the crown of the defeated king on his head, declaring that there was a new sheriff in town. This was a show of gaining authority by overcoming an enemy. In Revelation 4:10, there is the account of those casting their crowns before the throne of God.

This is just a thought here, but I wonder----where did they get these crowns? Could it be the conquests they won and the subsequent crowns from those victories? When individuals overcome an addiction, I believe they gain authority over the enemy.

Instead of using creative means to avoid confrontation with our weaknesses, why not overcome and gain new freedom along with greater authority? Blessing your mind to have the mind of Christ so you can overcome is a start. We have talked at length about blessing others; we should also look at blessing ourselves. Declare over yourself that you are a child of God who lacks for nothing and will see good days in the land of the living. Blessing what is weak in you through speaking God's intentions will provide opportunities to get free. That blockage is not there to keep you from success, it is there as an opportunity for conquest to gain the spoil.

Are You Covered?

Elusive success, unfulfilled promises, and dashed hopes seem to be their lot in life. These are the negative patterns that function in some of the lives that I occasionally come across. More often than not, something happens that sabotages their expectations. As a result, they back off and are reluctant to believe for anything more. Lowered expectations become the protection against such disappointments. What do you think causes expected goodness to be sabotaged? I believe these are rooted in the issues of covering and love. Obviously, not every negative happening that comes our way is related to being under a curse. Sometimes bad decisions have a way of making us feel cursed. Well, I am not referring to those kinds of issues. There are some who cannot find any relief or favor in their life. I am not one who blames the devil for every disappointment in life. I do believe there are people who may not be aware of generational oppression that comes by a curse.

"Like a sparrow is in flitting; like a swallow in its flying, so a curse without a cause does not alight." Proverbs 26:2

Remember, the definition for a curse: to place something in a lower position than what God intended. It is safe to say that one does not come under a curse casually or easily. Someone cursing you is not enough; there would need to be a point of acceptance through an open door. That pathway could be agreement by also cursing others, or maybe through fear that the curse has power over you. There are curses that come due to family members--- such as a father or grandfather--- being a part of cultic groups who take oaths against their own bodies and their children's children. Some cults may seem harmless on the surface, but when you read the oaths that affect their posterity they are anything but harmless. These oaths are not usually known by the family members, so it could be important to learn if you have had any close relatives involved in any type of organization of this type. Much freedom and favor comes when the cursing is reversed through blessing.

A Father's Responsibility

BLESS YOURSELF

Walk with me through a biblical account of a family where the issue of covering affected the generations that followed.

"Then Noah began farming and planted a vineyard. He drank of the wine and became drunk and uncovered himself inside his tent. Ham, the father of Canaan, saw the nakedness of his father and told his brothers outside. But Shem and Japeth took a garment and laid it upon both their shoulders and walked backward and covered the nakedness of their father; and their faces were turned away, so that they did not see their father's nakedness." Gen. 9:20-23

Noah began to rebuild life on earth. He made a vineyard, which also was another first recorded in the Bible. Enjoying the fruit was satisfying until Noah had too much wine and passed out naked in his tent. Along came Ham and saw his father exposed. Unaware that he was setting in motion unfortunate consequences for his lineage, Ham further exposed his father by telling his two brothers. His two brothers did the honorable thing and covered their father's nakedness immediately. No one else needed to witness Noah in his vulnerable moment. When sobered, Noah discovered what Ham had done, and Noah cursed Canaan (the son of Ham) by saying, "cursed be Canaan; a servant of servants he shall be to his brothers". (Gen. 9:25)

Notice it was Ham's son that received the curse, and the curse placed him lower than even a servant to serve his brothers. Noah blessed the two brothers for their honor in covering their father by saying;

> *"Blessed be the Lord, the God of Shem, and let Canaan be his servant. May God enlarge Japheth and let him dwell in the tents of Shem, and let Canaan be his servant."*
> Gen. 9:26-27

Uncovering someone is a serious matter in the eyes of God. Ham's sin was not in witnessing his father's nakedness, but in telling of what he saw. He could have easily covered his father's nakedness just as his brothers' did when they found out. Ham also violated a spiritual principle. Belittling a parent, dignitary, or anyone that is in a place of authority by making them appear foolish or look silly, places those doing the mocking in a lowered position. Ham was belittling and making Noah appear lower than what God intended him to be. Those doing the cursing may not realize that they are putting themselves in the place of the cursed. Remember, Jesus came to deliver and defend those who are under a curse. Someone deliberately cursing for sport will find themselves in opposition to the cross. Ham's action placed him in a cursed position and brought a curse on his lineage. The cause that brought a curse to Ham's family was his own dishonoring of the one who had authority over his life.

When is the telling of something gossip and when is it not? Gossip's sting is to expose someone for the purpose of turning the hearts of others away from them. One cannot be accused of gossip if they choose to bless as a way to turn the situation for good. If their desire is to turn the situation for something other than good, then the motive could not be from a heart of blessing. Informing someone who then has the ability and authority to help the situation for the good --- this is different.

"If anyone sees his brother committing a sin not leading to death, he shall ask, and God will for him give life."
1 John 5:16

John encourages us to ask God. By asking God in prayer to open their blinded eyes in whatever area it might be, rather than tell others of their failures. Choices fathers make will open or close doors to cursing. A father walking before the Lord in a righteous way (God's way) releases the blessing of the Lord to the third and fourth generation. A father will find it passed down, as in the case with Cain. (see Exod. 20:5) Turning to the Lord, however, reverses the curse and establishes the favor of the Lord. There is a strong thread throughout Scripture about the necessity of having mentors and spiritual fathers in our lives. Having Godly mentors and spiritual fathers can produce a healthy and proper perspective of authority.

Remember, the brothers who covered their father Noah, were not only blessed, but so were their offspring for generations to come. Neither they, nor their brother Ham ever imagined that their acts of covering or uncovering would lead to such drastic effects that would change their families for generations. Notice, the curser became the cursed and the blesser became the blessed. The one who covered and ultimately was blessed was also the one who became master to the one who did the uncovering or cursing.

Now, we are briefly introduced to Nimrod, a grandson of Ham, and someone whom the Bible called a "mighty hunter before the Lord". (Gen. 10:9) Nimrod built Babel. Does that sound familiar? Shinar was the Babylonian empire. Today, we would call it Iraq, Iran, and some of Saudi Arabia. All the other sons of Noah inhabited parts of the Middle East, Canaan, and Gaza. They were shepherds. There is a great difference between the heart of a shepherd and that of a hunter. A shepherd is one with a caring heart. David and Jesus are both referred to as shepherds. David was an actual Shepherd and Jesus was the Spiritual Shepherd of those lost through sin. A hunter stalks his prey through craftiness and camouflage. The contrast between these three brothers is worth noting. Their lives took on different perspectives and natures after the event of covering--- or in Ham's case, uncovering their father's nakedness, which brought on a blessing or a curse.

First One To Uncover

Lets revisit a heavenly event where Lucifer, an angel made to be a covering, became one that uncovers. It was the first act of rebellion against authority.

"You were in Eden, the garden of God, every precious stone was your covering; the ruby, the topaz, and the diamond; the beryl, the onyx and the jasper; the lapis laszuli, the turquoise and the emerald; and the gold, the workmanship

of your settings, and sockets, was in you. On the day that you were created they were prepared. You were the anointed cherub who covers, and I placed you there. You were on the holy mountain of God; you walked in the midst of stones of fire. You were blameless in your ways from the day you were created until unrighteousness was found in you. By the abundance of your trade you were internally filled with violence, and you sinned; therefore, I have cast you as a profane thing from the mountain of God. And I have destroyed you, O covering cherub, from the midst of the stones of fire." Ezekiel 28: 13-16

Lucifer was the angel created to oversee the sights and sounds of Heaven. In-built with gems and instruments, he was literally a walking orchestra. Few angels were privileged to enter the throne room of God, and Lucifer was one of them. His job was to cover and release the presence of God, and lead the angelic hosts in the worship of God. But something dark lurked in the recesses of his heart that corrupted him. Lucifer wanted to BE the one that was worshipped. Eventually that led him to conspire, and with a third of the angels, he made war against God ,the Creator Himself.

That day he moved from being a covering cherub to being an uncovering one. Exposing and uncovering the saints before the Lord became his new specialty. The fallen angel had become the devil and the "accuser (or curser) of the brethren". Yet God, who is all about covering and blessing, sent us the one who truly covers--- His Son Jesus Christ.

BLESS YOURSELF

Jesus' shed blood became the covering and cleansing from sin. Jesus' blood, placed upon the Mercy Seat in Heaven, not only covered us, but also cleansed us. The devil will do anything to introduce us to cursing. Working against a relationship, the enemy attempts to weaken those ties by tempting us to uncover each other. Everyone will need the covering grace of God at some point in our lives.

CHAPTER 20

OUR HEAVENLY FATHER IS A BLESSER

We have come to the final part of our journey in what blessing others is all about. I could go on and on with many more stories, testimonies, and teaching on this subject because it branches into every area and aspect of our lives.

I will conclude this teaching by going back to the Garden of Eden where the first curse took place. Our Heavenly Father is a Blesser. So when He created Adam and Eve, He made them in His image. That means they also were created to be blessers. When Lucifer entered the picture, he tempted them and they sinned. Immediately Adam committed the first act by human kind to curse another. He first cursed God himself by blaming Him for giving him a woman. She in turn continued to do the same. From then on, man has fallen into the same deception and has become an expert in the art of cursing (uncovering, accusing) instead of blessing others by the spoken word.

OUR HEAVENLY FATHER IS A BLESSER

" And so it is written, the first man Adam, was made a living soul; the last Adam was made a quickening spirit. Howbeit that was not first which is spiritual, but that which is natural; and afterward that which is spiritual. The first man is of the earth, earthy; the second man (Jesus) is The Lord from Heaven." 1 Cor. 15:45-47

Jesus is the Head of the Church, whom He loves and blesses, and so should every husband follow in the footsteps of The Lord. The husband should bless his wife and children as God does His bride and His children. God wants to restore the gift of blessing to our families as He intended from the beginning. A wife and children follow the example of the husband. Nothing covers like love. I am referring to the kind of love that covers a multitude of sins, the Agape kind of love. God's kind of love does not expose weakness. His kind of love is a Spirit. Without God's kind of love on the earth, there would be anarchy to the point that there would be no restraint or self-control of any kind. Humankind left alone is destructive, and very self-indulgent. One of God's reasons for marriage is to teach us how to walk in His unselfish and unconditional love. He said, " it is not good that man should be alone".

"Man left by himself is very self-indulgent and self-centered." Gen. 2:18

God's kind of love is not a feeling or an emotion. His love is constant and is not based on whether we deserve it. His love is without respect of person and is willing to lay down

OUR HEAVENLY FATHER IS A BLESSER

his life (his selfish needs and intentions) for others.

"Above all, keep fervent in your love for one another, because love covers a multitude of sins." 1 Peter 4:8

The word fervent here means without ceasing. We are to love with that kind of intensity. Mediocrity, the enemy of excellence, is given an open door to enter when we do not love fervently. I think mediocrity can be a curse that is caught like the flu from another family member. Relationships require work and time, and the neglect of said relationships will slowly erode them until one wonders what went wrong.

A marriage is the perfect picture of how Jesus cares for His Bride, The Church. The New Testament covenant is lived out through this mystery of love. What makes this mystery work is that someone is willing to die to his or her own selfishness. Marriage is the most unselfish act we will ever do. It requires thought and deliberate actions, while being more conscious of the needs and welfare of the one you love than yourself.

" Husbands, love your wives, just as Christ loved the church and gave Himself up for her: so that He might sanctify her (put her in a special place of honor) having cleansed her with the washing of water with The Word."
Ephesians 5:25-26

In other words, if I may paraphrase, He speaks to us from His Word, things that edify or bless, and encourage us, instead of words that tear us down by uncovering and discouraging us. It is important to note how Jesus cleanses His bride. He does so by washing her with His Word. The power of His Word washes away the effects of all others. When someone wounds a spouse, there is nothing more potent than the words of blessing that come from a husband or wife. A husband who blesses his wife strenghthens the cords of the marriage covenant . The power of blessing is the power of love. God so loved the world that He gave His Son to bless the Church. We have the kind of spouse we bless or the kind we curse, either by covering (blessing) or uncovering (cursing).

    A pastor and brother in Christ, whom I will call Terry, (not his real name) shared this encounter that he had with a man one day when he had been invited to minister at another church. It was right after the service and Terry was in a hurry to get on the road to his next engagement. The pastor asked him if he would talk to a man who was very upset. Pastor Terry told him that he didn't have much time, but he would give a few minutes. Neither of them knew the man, but he began by saying that his wife was at the lawyer's office at that moment filing for divorce.

He explained that he had been working in Iraq as a Christian contractor. He quickly told them how ungrateful she was and how being away for extended periods of time was the only way he could stay with her. His anger was vindictive, without any obvious brokenness for the situation. He made the usual accusations and blame. Terry stopped him and said, "Sir, you are a curser, and your marriage reflects the kind of wife you have been cursing". He was angry at the statement and told him he had studied various forms of martial arts and could throw him against the wall just by using his mind. He concluded by saying that he must get on the road, but he gave him some CD's that would help. They were on The Power of The Tongue, and then he left.

Pastor Terry had the opportunity to be in Houston the next month, and to his surprise, this same man came up to him and said, "Do you remember me"? Pastor Terry thought to himself, "Yes I do. You are the man who wanted to throw me against the wall with your mind". He acknowledged that he did remember him. This time he had a smile on his face, and his demeanor was noticeably different. Again, his first thought was, he has found someone else. He motioned for a lady to come over to him where they were. He placed his arm around her and said, "this is my wife of twenty-eight years". Terry asked, "What has happened since I saw you last"? The man said, "I reluctantly listened to the teaching you gave me. When my wife came home from the office, I met her in the hallway and I blessed her using some of the language suggested in the teaching'.

His wife described what it was like. She said, "It was strange because it was as if the words were tangible and moving in slow motion when they hit her heart". She explained the feeling was like liquid love flowing through her body, again the power of the washing of the word. They both agreed, that last month was like the honeymoon they never had. They now understand the power of blessing that can turn a potential divorce into a covenant of love. Jesus said, " it is the Spirit who gives life, the flesh profits nothing; the words that I have spoken to you are spirit and are life". (John 6:63) The cleansing words of blessing can change a heart set on destruction to restoration.

Love does not expose the vulnerability and weaknesses of men. Marriages today show evidence of the enmy's work of division in the home through subtle cursing in humor or sarcasm. I have listened to husbands and wives at various social gatherings use sarcasm to ridicule their spouse's cooking or their looks just to get a laugh at the expense of their spouse. I understand everyone has their own dynamic in their family and this kind of humor may be introduced and accepted. What I was referring to is the kind that tears down through uncovering a weakness in another. What they don't realize is that they are cursing their own flesh. A man's union with his wife is a covenant agreement that must be upheld and protected. Men, you can have this blessing your wife with a sincere heart through the washing of words that bring life to her heart. A husband is to follow the example of Jesus. Jesus first loved us His bride (He took the first step) by dying for us by the washing of His Word. He became the living Word and brings life to our spirit. His Word edifies, strengthens, builds up and covers a multitude of sins. We mean more to Him than His own life.

(1 Peter 3:7) " You husbands in the same way, live with your wives in an understanding way, as with someone weaker (her heart feels the impact of words deeper) since she is a woman;

and show her honor as a fellow heir of the grace of life (she is your spiritual sister and flesh of your flesh) so that your prayers are not hindered".

That is the way God created her so that you may learn what power you have in the words you speak to either damage or heal and strengthen your bond with her., as Christ does the Church. Men, God hears your prayers and is ready to bless your marriage, but when you dishonor and disrespect your wife, He cannot, because you are cursing and not blessing her. God is a blesser. We are created in His image; He blesses us, His bride, His Church, His wife, and we are responsive to Him.

The word " hinder" in this passage is expecto. I learned the meaning of this word from my friend Pastor Terry, He said expecto means "to frustrate or to cut down". The idea is one who keeps chopping down a tree that he expects good fruit to come from. If we want the fruit of love, joy, and peace to come from the marriage, we have to stop chopping at the tree. In the same sense, praying is frustrated when husbands are tearing down their wife while believing for their prayer to be answered. Submission is not a problem when a husband is blessing his wife as Christ would His Bride, the Church. Submission means to come under the mission. Men, you need to know what the mission is so your wife can come under the mission. The mission is simple---to love The Lord God with all our heart, mind and strength, and to show forth His goodness through marriage. What woman would have trouble living under the banner of love?

OUR HEAVENLY FATHER IS A BLESSER

Our Heavenly Father does not compete with His Church. He is not insecure. When we are born again, we are made one with Him. He is the head of His body. He compliments, encourages, and uplifts us. He blesses us and is not threatened by our gifts and callings. He is blessed by the fruits we have that reflect back on Him because they are a help to His body. Does the right hand compete with the left? No, they each have their strengths and contribute to help make the body stronger. In the head is the brain, and whatever the head chooses to allow in it will either bless the body or curse it. Such is the assignment of the husband over his wife and children. God is truth. Bless and be blessed, curse and be cursed.

Some men grow up in families where exposing one's wife and her weaknesses is an art form. Family reunions are occasions for the men to become experts at who can put down their wife using sarcasm. It isn't much fun for the wife, and in some cases, the husband, because it is uncovering or tearing down trust that a wife has for her husband or a husband for his wife. God has placed a husband in the position to initiate the blessing, just as He initiates the blessing over us. We love Him because he first loved us. A woman needs security, just as we the Church need security in Him. Not just the physical protection of her husband, but spiritual, emotional and mental security. Cursing will cease in a family when it is no longer fed. A husband who threatens his wife with threats of abandoning her or who uses money as tactical blackmail, needs to understand that a curse comes right back on them for the emotional abuse. I know that some of you may be thinking that this is all on the backs of men. Concerning marriage, the bible speaks two thirds more to men than women in the New Testament.

    Men, satan, knows that if you get understanding in being the blesser of your wife, you will have victory in your marriage. He doesn't want you to know this, so if you want to give the devil what he deserves, become a blesser. Trust your Creator. I think God has a pretty good idea of how to make your life at home your own Garden of Eden....after all, He wrote the original book of blessings. When there is an environment of blessing in the home, the children, too, will be at peace and will follow suit in honoring their mother and father. Children can set up their future by learning to bless their parents. Men, it is never too late. If your children are grown and out, they will still observe how you treat your wife and their mother. It's never too late for them to learn. Don't let satan lie to you. Don't allow him to steal from you anymore. He is an expert at causing division. If he can cause division between a husband and wife, then he has succeeded to destroy your home. Start today to become a blesser. You can reverse the curse. The Bible exhorts children to honor their mother and their father so that it will go well with them and they will live long on the earth; this is the first commandment with a promise.

    One of the best compliments I have ever received came from one of my children, " Thank you for teaching us all the things you taught us, and thank you for always being there for us. You still hold true to what you believe without wavering through the years".

Those words mean the world to me because I know that I made a lot of mistakes (as we all do) along the way, but only my steadfastness on the truth of God's Word was the focus. Thank you Jesus! When you choose to follow His plan according to the revelation knowledge that you have at the time, He is faithfull to His Word and is there for you. You can't go wrong with Him as your teacher and guide. I want my children to know that I have not wavered from the first day that I said, " I love Jesus". The words of blessing coming from your children can enlarge your heart and capacity to love like nothing else will. Love is not an idea; it is required when ministering the gifts of the Spirit.

"Pursue love, yet desire earnestly spiritual gifts, but especially that you may prophecy." 1 Cor.14:1

The apostle Paul makes a distinction between pursuing and desiring. In pursuing love, there is effort involved. It implies there is some premeditated thought and planning involved. Desire, by contrast, is a willingness that is hidden and waiting for opportunity. Pursuit implies that opportunity is provided, as the action of love becomes a step of faith. Blessing, like love, is a choice of pursuit that is planned for and then the desire catches up with the pursuit. Pursuing love is simply pursuing the things that reveal the character of the Lord in the relationship. The Bible teaches us that love covers a multitude of sins. Love truly seeks to cover the faults of others. If we will not be reactive to bad news and will indeed be proactive with blessing, things can quickly turn around in our favor. Bless with awareness that your words are powerful.

OUR HEAVENLY FATHER IS A BLESSER

Life and death are in the tongue. Actually, they begin in the heart, and out of the abundance of the heart they are sown. Backhanded compliments, no matter how cleverly disguised, are still deadly. Knowing that what we speak takes on a spiritual life should be enough to make us choose to bless.

"And He led them as far as Bethany, and He lifted up His hands and blessed them. While He was blessing them, He parted from them and was carried up into Heaven."
Luke 24:50-51

Those were Jesus' final moments on the earth. Hands lifted up, He blessed the disciples. This was the Aaronic blessing. It is interesting to note Jesus' last act on earth before He ascended was to bless.

What a way to go; to end one's ministry with blessing. I try to start each day with speaking a blessing over my husband, our children, grandchildren, God's people, our spiritual family and myself. Then, before I go to bed, I end my day in the same way. When you blame another for your problem, your soul has become their slave. To begin to see yourself and the world around you through God's eyes means that our vision must be holy and transformed by Him.

Sealing this teaching with a blessing to the finale. I speak God's manifold blessings over you as you apply living with blessing instead of cursing. Speaking God's language.

OUR HEAVENLY FATHER IS A BLESSER

LET'S PRAY

Father, we thank You for what You are doing and saying to us in these last days. We want to be a covering Church; a covering mother and father. We want to be fathers who know how to love our children. We want to be husbands who understand how to cover our wives. Lord, any areas where we have not been faithful in covering others, we ask you to forgive us now. We know that Your Word declares that a child who does not honor their parents cuts their life short. We understand and recognize that when we rightly discern the Lord's Body, we will have good health and long life (see 1Cor.11:29-30). Lord, bring to mind areas we need to cover in blessing. We pray that we would have a new standard in our lives, which is, " I bless you in the name of the Lord, and I bless you coming in, and I bless you going out". We pray that our children and grandchildren will carry blessing and they will have the favor of The Lord from teachers, bosses, and dignitaries. Lord, we pray You would survey our lives and show us where we have sabotaged favor through cursing. Father, we come under Your covering just as Ruth positioned herself at the feet of her Redeemer, and He stretched out His mantle and covered her. Thank You for the covering of The Lord Jesus, for when the enemy sees the blood, he has to pass over us. You cover our homes and lives for which we are grateful. We pray Lord that words of life and spirit will flow out of husbands toward their wives and wives toward their husbands. Anoint us, Holy Spirit, to speak over one another with words that are creative, for You have created us to walk and talk in Your image. Amen.

OUR HEAVENLY FATHER IS A BLESSER

"And there shall be no more curse; but the throne of God and of The lamb shall be in it; and His servants shall serve Him." Revelation 22:3

Your Heavenly Father is the redemptive God who delights in bringing things back into His divine order. Learning how to bless, you can participate in this redemptive process. By actively living a lifestyle of blessing, you will see changes in the hearts of those you bless----as well as yourself!

Finally dear friend, we have to confess our sins in order to be born again of the Spirit and to inherit the blessings. Ask Jesus Christ the Son of the living God to come into your heart right now. He loves you and is waiting for you to cry out to Him.

"That if thou shalt confess with the mouth the Lord Jesus, and shalt believe in thine heart that God hath raised Him from the dead, thou shalt be saved. For with the heart man believeth unto righteousness; and with the mouth confession is made into salvation." Romans 10: 9,10

SALVATION PRAYER

Jesus, I ask You to come into my heart. I confess You as my Lord and Savior, and I believe that You have risen from the dead.

God Bless you.